WAFFLES

•:•: Sweet, Savory, Simple •:•:

Dawn Yanagihara
Photographs by Lucy Schaeffer

CHRONICLE BOOKS
SAN FRANCISCO

Library of Congress Cataloging-in-Publication Data
available.

ISBN 978-1-4521-0703-5

Manufactured in China
Designed by Michael Morris
Text and recipes by Dawn Yanagihara
Food styling by Adrienne Anderson
Prop styling by Martha Bernabe
Typesetting by Donna Linden

10 9 8 7 6 5 4 3 2

Chronicle Books LLC
680 Second Street
San Francisco, California 94107
www.chroniclebooks.com

CONTENTS

INTRODUCTION

In one of my oversimplified views of human beings, there are two types of people: those who like pancakes and those who like waffles. Pancake people are the constants—salt-of-the-earth, get-things-done folks who are stable, grounded, even-tempered, in control, and otherwise as level as pancakes are flat and floppy. Waffle people, on the other hand—of which I am one—are off-kilter, willy-nilly, moody, irascible, easily distracted, and subject to experiencing peaks and valleys, like those that define a waffle.

This is mostly nonsense, of course. But here's a truth: when it comes to waffles and pancakes, I've yet to meet anyone who likes one as much as the other. If you're reading this, you're probably a wafflephile to some degree. Like me, you love waffles for their crisp surfaces that conceal a tender, airy crumb; for their ingenious pockets that keep anything put on top from slipping onto the plate; for their ability to soak up butter and syrup yet retain their texture; and for their all-around toothsomeness and charm.

Waffles have been so fully integrated into the American way of eating that it's hard *not* to think that they were born and bred in the good ol' US of A. But they are, in fact, European in provenance and older than our nation itself. What we know as waffles today are descendents of wafers made in the Middle Ages using hinged plates held over an open fire; indeed, the word *waffle* is rooted in the word *wafer*. Waffles—or knowledge of them—are said to have crossed the Atlantic with the first English settlers in North America, who became acquainted with the food during time spent in Holland. Over the centuries that followed, waffles gained in popularity, and

at long last, in the early 20th century, the first electric waffle iron came off the assembly line, a blessing to all waffle-loving souls. But Belgian waffles—yeast-risen waffles of stature—didn't debut in America until 1964 at the New York World's Fair. Needless to say, they were very well received.

This brings up the point that there are two types of waffles: the quick, American-engineered waffle leavened with baking powder and/or baking soda, and the old-world yeasted waffle (also called a raised waffle) that requires several hours of rising time. Quick waffles are, well, fast to make and are terrific for that fact alone. Yeasted waffles have a lighter, more ethereal texture and a more complex flavor from the yeast's fermentation, but putting them on the table requires some forethought. Both can taste stupendous.

This little book offers more than thirty excellent waffle recipes—if I do say so myself—plus a choice of topping options. Quick waffles are the focus, but a couple of yeasted waffles are here too. You'll find trusty, basic waffles—ones that any waffle compendium is obliged to include—as well as some that might surprise you and a few that might alter the way you think about these honeycombed delights. There are sweet recipes, savory recipes, and sweet-and-savory recipes that deliver winsome waffles for any time of the day and each course of a meal, including dessert. So unpack your new waffle iron or dust off your old one and let's go convert some of those pancake people!

INGREDIENTS

One of the great things about waffles is that many types can be made with refrigerator and pantry staples. The ingredients mentioned here are used regularly in recipes throughout this book.

BAKING POWDER AND BAKING SODA

All but two of the waffle batters in these pages call for chemical leavening: baking powder, baking soda, or a combination of both. These two types of leaveners serve the same purpose but are reactive in different ways, so take care not to mix them up when measuring (a mistake all bakers have made at some point). Make sure that your baking powder is fresh—check the date on the can or test it by stirring a spoonful into a cup of warm water. It should bubble and fizz energetically.

BUTTER

The recipes in this book that call for butter—and that's most of them—specify unsalted butter. Using unsalted butter allows you to carefully control the saltiness of your food. This is especially important when baking—including when making waffles—because with baked goods, unlike when making, say, a pot of soup, it's impossible to taste for seasoning as you go, and to add more seasoning at the table.

BUTTERMILK

Buttermilk today may be commercially cultured, and not the by-product of churning fresh cream into butter that it was in the past, but it's still quite a magical ingredient. Its acidity and temperate richness do amazing things for dishes of all sorts—from waffles to fried chicken. Buttermilk is available in low-fat and nonfat

varieties; either will work in these recipes, but the low-fat type will yield better-tasting results because of the bit of butterfat it contains. Buttermilk curdles easily if overwarmed, so if you're trying to bring it to room temperature in a microwave oven, heat it at 30 or 40 percent power in short 15-second increments, checking and stirring before going another round.

CORNMEAL

For waffles with a delicate crunch rather than a gritty, pebbly texture, use finely ground cornmeal, not coarsely ground or even medium ground. And for the best-tasting results, use whole-grain cornmeal, which owes its fullness of flavor to the fact that the germ is intact when the corn is milled. Whole-grain cornmeal is often stone ground, and is sold as such.

EGGS

All of the recipes in this book call for large eggs.

FLOUR

The recipes calling for flour were all developed using unbleached all-purpose flour. I find that this type of flour has a more wholesome and wheaty flavor than its bleached counterpart, which has been subjected to chemical treatment to lighten its color. However, feel free to use bleached all-purpose flour in its place, if that's what you have on hand.

MILK

Whole milk is the first choice when making waffle batter because it has just the right amount of richness. You can substitute low-fat milk, with some sacrifice in flavor (if I do this, I usually increase the butter a bit just to up the fat content). I advise against using non-fat milk; it's simply too lean.

NUTS

Nuts are always better after they've been toasted—their texture is crisper and their flavor fuller. You can spread them in a single layer on a baking sheet and toast them in a 350°F/180°C/gas 4 oven for 8 to 10 minutes until they're browned and fragrant, but I've burned many batches of nuts this way because, as the saying goes, out of sight, out of mind. With the exception of hazelnuts, which benefit from all-encompassing oven heat to loosen their skins, I prefer to toast nuts and shredded coconut in a frying pan over medium to medium-high heat, stirring occasionally, until fragrant and browned. Let cool completely before use.

SALT

At the risk of sounding pretentious—this is a book about waffles, after all—I've called for fine sea salt throughout, simply because I prefer to use minimally processed ingredients. Of course, regular table salt works perfectly well in place of fine sea salt. If you're a user of kosher salt, you're probably savvy to the fact that you need to use roughly twice the amount of kosher salt as fine salt to get the same degree of salinity. When using kosher salt in baked goods, after measuring, I like to rub the crystals between my fingers to crush them so that they have better dispersal and dissolve more readily.

Taking Measure

Compared to other baked goods, waffles aren't a fussy lot. Their batters adapt quite well to small hiccups in ingredient measurements. A little too much flour? Not a problem. An extra splash of milk? No big deal. But for consistently good results, it might help to know that the recipes in this book were developed using the dip-and-sweep method for measuring dry ingredients: dip the dry measuring cup into, say, sugar, scoop up enough so that the sugar is mounded above the rim, and then level off the top with a straight edge, such as an icing spatula or the back of a table knife. In the case of flour, first fluff up the flour before dipping so that it will not wind up too tightly compressed in the cup.

A WORD ABOUT WAFFLE IRONS, BAKING TIMES, AND YIELDS

There are classic waffle makers, Belgian wafflers, heart-shaped machines, and "professional" flip-over contraptions that produce Belgian waffles with extra-deep pockets. A standard classic or Belgian model bakes individual round waffles about 6½ in/16.5 cm in diameter; a family-size waffler might produce six smallish square waffles at a time. Some machines, like my classic waffler, run hot; others, like my flip-over Belgian maker, run cool. Still others, such as my regular Belgian waffle iron, have both quick- and slow-baking settings.

All this is to say that with so many variables in waffle irons, baking times and yields are difficult to standardize. Some recipes in this book say to bake the waffles to your desired degree of doneness, but other waffles are at their best when baked especially dark, and when that is the case, I have made notes to this effect in the recipes. I've used the most common size of waffle iron, which turns out 6½-in/16.5-cm round waffles, to set the yield standard, so the number of waffles that each recipe yields is based on waffles of this size. Recipes in the Savories and Waffle Finales chapters that call for already made waffles use these standard-size waffles. If your machine makes waffles of a different size, use your judgment when it comes to portioning and serving sizes.

Have to Halve?

Many of the waffle recipes in this book make about eight standard waffles. If this seems like too many, keep in mind that more often than not, the first waffle is a test one that ends up misshapen or unevenly baked—fine for nibbling in the kitchen but perhaps not worthy of serving. In addition, leftovers can be frozen and reheated with almost no sacrifice in flavor or texture (see Tips for Successful Waffling, page 12). If a full recipe is still overkill, any recipe calling for two eggs can be halved, as long as you're willing to do some calculations for those ingredients that are not easily divisible.

TIPS FOR SUCCESSFUL WAFFLING

Baking waffles is about as easy and foolproof as baking gets. But still, here are a few pointers for achieving waffle greatness from this waffle baker, who has made scores upon scores of batches.

WAKE, MAKE, AND BAKE

In other words, mix the batter and get waffling right away. Waffle batters that contain baking powder or baking soda for leavening—and that's all but two of the batters in this book—can't be kept overnight in the refrigerator, because the leavening agents will lose their oomph and the waffles will bake up flat and dense. If you're aiming to minimize the amount of work required in the morning, have the dry ingredients mixed and ready to go so that all you'll need to do in the A.M. is combine the liquids and then mix the batter. Or opt for a yeasted waffle (see Belgian Waffles on page 22 or Anadama Waffles with Currants on page 44) with a batter that *must* be made at least 12 hours or up to 24 hours in advance.

SPREAD IT AROUND

Some waffle batters are thin and pourable in consistency. Others are thick and spreadable. A pourable batter usually does a fine job of distributing itself in the waffle grid once the lid is closed. A thick batter, however, needs some assistance: use a rubber spatula to push the batter to the edge of the waffle iron and smooth out the surface. Very thick batters should be spread to about ¼ in/6 mm of the perimeter, merely thick batters to about ½ in/12 mm.

GO FOR DEEP GOLD

A pale, barely golden waffle is not living up to its full potential, and that's a shame. Waffles need to be nicely browned for a couple of reasons. First, for texture. A deep golden brown color is visually appealing, yes, but it also means that the waffle's surface is crisp and will contrast beautifully with a moist and tender interior. The second reason is flavor. Browning creates flavor compounds in foods of all types, and waffles are no exception. A bronzed color is absolutely essential for rich, great-tasting, palate-pleasing waffles that are full of depth and complexity. To that end, I never bake any waffle on a setting lower than medium.

WHAT'S DONE ISN'T ALWAYS DONE

The waffle iron's dinging, chirping, or other signal doesn't necessarily mean that the waffle within is ready for removal. In fact, it rarely is. Open the lid and check on the browning. If the waffle isn't done, close the lid and continue cooking for as long as you'd like. There's no harm in extending the baking time, but don't get distracted, as I sometimes do, and forget about the waffle until your nose tells you it's too late.

BOTTOMS UP

It's not uncommon for the bottom side of a waffle to be more attractive than the top, so if the top surface is spotty brown or otherwise not up to par, simply flip the waffle as you remove it from the waffle iron. Or if you're intent on righting the wrong, flip the waffle, fit it back into the grid, and close the lid to continue baking and even out the browning.

COOL, BRIEFLY, FOR CRISPNESS . . .

Hot off the iron, a waffle has a slightly moist surface from all the steam that's released during baking. Allowing the waffle to cool for 30 to 60 seconds on a wire rack before serving gives the surface a chance to dry so that the waffle is crisp. Or see the next tip for an alternative approach.

OR KEEP THEM TOASTY

If you prefer to serve waffles all at once rather than one at a time as they come off the iron, place the baked waffles on a wire rack set over a rimmed baking sheet in a 225°F/110°C/gas ¼ oven. This will keep the waffles warm and, at the same time, crisp up their surfaces beautifully. Try not to exceed 15 to 20 minutes of holding time; the waffles will eventually begin to dry out too much and harden.

CRYOGENICS

Waffles keep remarkably well in the freezer. Once they're cool, stack them up; seal them in a zipper-lock bag, pressing out as much air as possible; and toss the bag into the freezer. If you're so inclined, placing a square of waxed or parchment paper between the waffles in the stack will make it extra-easy to separate them when frozen, but I almost never bother with this step. Waffles can be kept frozen for up to two months.

REVIVING YOUR WAFFLES

To rewarm and recrisp a frozen waffle, put it straight from the freezer into a toaster or toaster oven, and give it a couple of rounds on a low setting so that the center warms through and the exterior crisps without scorching. If you need to heat several frozen waffles at once, lay them out on a rack set over a baking sheet and place in a 375°F/190°C/gas 5 or 400°F/200°C/gas 6 oven for 8 to 10 minutes, turning the waffles once halfway through.

CHAPTER 1
WAFFLES PLAIN AND SIMPLE

When the craving for waffles comes on, chances are that it's a basic, no-nonsense waffle you're wanting, the sort that mom dished out on Sunday morning to hungry mouths, the type that comes together with very little fuss or forethought with ingredients you have on hand. Such waffles may be plain and simple, but there's still lots to love: their deep golden color, delicate crispness, and light moist crumb. And their flavor, too—toasty, wheaty, and subtly sweet, with just a touch of saltiness. They're tasty on their own, but toppings make them even better.

In this chapter, you'll find recipes for those basic waffles that we all know and love. "Basic," however, does not mean boring or average or middling in quality. In fact, three of my all-time favorite waffles—ones that I think are exemplary of their kind—are right here in this group: the lovely, airy, yeasted Belgian Waffles, the wonderfully crisp and corny Golden Cornmeal Waffles, and the deliciously fragrant and utterly irresistible Malted Waffles.

CLASSIC WAFFLES

These waffles may be basic, but they're solidly, dependably good, with just enough sugar for sweetness, baking powder for lift, and butter for richness. The batter comes together quickly, with ingredients that you probably have on hand. The cornstarch, a bit of an oddity in the ingredient lineup, helps keep the waffles supremely light and tender, but you can choose to leave it out—just be sure to use a gentle hand when mixing the batter.

INGREDIENTS

2	cups/280 g unbleached all-purpose flour
2	tbsp sugar
1½	tbsp cornstarch (optional)
2½	tsp baking powder
1	tsp fine sea salt
2	large eggs
2	cups/480 ml whole milk, at room temperature
6	tbsp/85 g unsalted butter, melted and cooled slightly

If you plan to hold the waffles and serve them all at once rather than one at a time hot off the waffle iron, preheat the oven to 225°F/110°C/gas ¼ and set a large wire rack on a large, rimmed baking sheet.

Preheat your waffle iron.

In a large bowl, whisk together the flour, sugar, cornstarch (if using), baking powder, and salt until well combined.

In a medium bowl, whisk the eggs until combined, and then whisk in the milk. Gradually whisk in the butter.

Pour the liquid ingredients into the dry ingredients and whisk gently just until the batter is evenly moistened. It's fine if some small lumps remain. Give the batter a couple of folds with a rubber spatula to ensure that there aren't any pockets of flour.

Pour a generous ½ cup/120 ml of the batter (or the waffler manufacturer's recommended amount) into the center of the waffle iron. Use the rubber spatula to even it out and distribute it slightly (but there is no need to spread it all the way to the edges). Close the lid and bake the waffle to the desired doneness.

Remove the waffle and serve it immediately before baking the remaining batter. Or set it on the wire rack and slide the baking sheet into the oven to keep the waffle warm. Bake the remaining batter, transferring each waffle to the rack in the oven.

BUTTERMILK WAFFLES

MAKES ABOUT **8** **STANDARD (6½-IN/16.5-CM) ROUND WAFFLES**

In these waffles, the buttermilk doesn't taste tangy. Rather, its tartness translates to a full, hearty flavor that's not found in most sweet-milk waffles. Hot off the iron, the waffles are lightly crisp (especially if they're left in the iron for a few seconds longer than the point at which the waffler indicates they're done) and their interiors are moist and supple—a pleasing contrast in textures. Buttermilk waffles pair seamlessly with just about any type of topping, and are great used in savory preparations.

INGREDIENTS

1¾	cups/250 g unbleached all-purpose flour
2½	tbsp sugar
1¾	tsp baking powder
¾	tsp fine sea salt
¼	tsp baking soda
2	large eggs, separated
2	cups/480 ml buttermilk, at room temperature
6	tbsp/85 g unsalted butter, melted and cooled slightly

If you plan to hold the waffles and serve them all at once rather than one at a time hot off the waffle iron, preheat the oven to 225°F/110°C/gas ¼ and set a large wire rack on a large, rimmed baking sheet.

Preheat your waffle iron.

In a large bowl, whisk together the flour, sugar, baking powder, salt, and baking soda until well combined.

In a medium bowl, whisk the egg yolks until combined, and then whisk in the buttermilk. Gradually whisk in the butter.

Pour the liquid ingredients into the dry ingredients and whisk gently just until the batter is evenly moistened. It's fine if some small lumps remain. The batter will be quite thick.

In a clean medium bowl, with a clean whisk, rotary beater, or handheld mixer, beat the egg whites until they hold soft peaks. Using a rubber spatula, slide the beaten whites onto the batter and gently fold them in.

Pour a generous ½ cup/120 ml of the batter (or the waffler manufacturer's recommended amount) into the center of the waffle iron. Use the rubber spatula to even it out and distribute it slightly (but there's no need to spread it all the way to the edges). Close the lid and bake the waffle to the desired doneness. (I like to let these waffles go for an additional 15 to 20 seconds after the indicator light says they're done, to heighten their crispness.)

Remove the waffle and serve it immediately before baking the remaining batter. Or set it on the wire rack and slide the baking sheet into the oven to keep the waffle warm. Bake the remaining batter, transferring each waffle to the rack in the oven. (The batter will thicken as it sits. This is perfectly normal. Don't thin it out with additional liquid.)

MALTED WAFFLES

MAKES ABOUT **8** **STANDARD (6½-IN/16.5-CM) ROUND WAFFLES**

Hands down, these are the best-smelling waffles. Ever. You know that amazing fragrance that fills an ice cream shop that bakes homemade cones? That same intoxicating aroma will fill your kitchen when you bake this batter. Many malted waffles are so light on malt that it's hard to detect the malt flavor. Not so with these. It's important, however, to use the correct type of malt—you'll need nondiastatic malt powder, not diastatic malt powder (which is used in bread production) or malted milk powder (which contains ingredients like sugar and powdered milk in addition to malt powder). Nondiastatic malt powder is sold in many natural foods stores and, of course, can be ordered online. I adore these waffles, so I think making the effort to procure some is well worth it.

INGREDIENTS

2	cups/280 g unbleached all-purpose flour
¾	cup/90 g nondiastatic malt powder
1½	tbsp sugar
2¼	tsp baking powder
1	tsp fine sea salt
2	large eggs
2	cups/480 ml whole milk, at room temperature
½	tsp vanilla extract
6	tbsp/85 g unsalted butter, melted and cooled slightly

If you plan to hold the waffles and serve them all at once rather than one at a time hot off the waffle iron, preheat the oven to 225°F/110°C/gas ¼ and set a large wire rack on a large, rimmed baking sheet.

Preheat your waffle iron.

In a large bowl, whisk together the flour, malt powder, sugar, baking powder, and salt until well combined.

In a medium bowl, whisk the eggs until combined, and then whisk in the milk and vanilla. Gradually whisk in the butter.

Pour the liquid ingredients into the dry ingredients and whisk gently just until the batter is evenly moistened. It's fine if some small lumps remain. Give the batter a couple of folds with a rubber spatula to ensure that there aren't any pockets of flour.

Pour a generous ½ cup/120 ml of the batter (or the waffler manufacturer's recommended amount) into the center of the waffle iron. Use the rubber spatula to even it out and distribute it slightly (but there's no need to spread it all the way to the edges). Close the lid and bake the waffle to the desired doneness.

Remove the waffle and serve it immediately before baking the remaining batter. Or set it on the wire rack and slide the baking sheet into the oven to keep the waffle warm. Bake the remaining batter, transferring each waffle to the rack in the oven. (The batter will thicken a bit as it sits. This is perfectly normal. Don't thin it out with additional liquid.)

GOLDEN CORNMEAL WAFFLES

A high-quality, fine-textured, stone-ground cornmeal (sometimes called whole-grain cornmeal) delivers the fullest, sweetest corn flavor, replete with nutty, mineral-y notes. It makes all the difference in the world in these waffles. And with a subtle crystalline crunch from the cornmeal and light (but not featherweight) crumb from the beaten egg whites, these waffles are one of my all-time favorites. Each waffle emerges from the iron deep golden in color, but its delicate crispness is at its best if the waffle is allowed to cool for a minute on a wire rack before serving. Cornmeal waffles are sublime with plain maple syrup, but Blueberry Compote (page 94) or Molasses-Orange Butter (page 88) would be great as well. They reheat like superstars, so don't hesitate to keep extras in the freezer.

INGREDIENTS	
1⅓	cups/200 g fine stone-ground (whole-grain) yellow cornmeal
1	cup/140 g unbleached all-purpose flour
2½	tbsp sugar
1¾	tsp baking powder
1	tsp fine sea salt
¼	tsp baking soda
2	large eggs, separated
2⅓	cups/555 ml buttermilk, at room temperature
6	tbsp/85 g unsalted butter, melted and cooled slightly

If you plan to serve the waffles as you make them, set a wire rack beside the waffle iron for cooling each one briefly before serving. If you plan to hold the waffles and serve them all at once rather than one at a time, preheat the oven to 225°F/110°C/gas ¼ and set a large wire rack on a large, rimmed baking sheet.

Preheat your waffle iron.

In a large bowl, whisk together the cornmeal, flour, sugar, baking powder, salt, and baking soda until well combined.

In a medium bowl, whisk the egg yolks and buttermilk until combined. Gradually whisk in the butter.

Pour the liquid ingredients into the dry ingredients and whisk gently just until the batter is evenly moistened. It's fine if some small lumps remain. The batter will be quite thick.

In a clean medium bowl, with a clean whisk, rotary beater, or handheld mixer, beat the egg whites until they hold soft peaks. Using a rubber spatula, slide the beaten whites onto the batter and gently fold them in.

Pour a generous ½ cup/120 ml of the batter (or the waffler manufacturer's recommended amount) into the center of the waffle iron. Use the rubber spatula to spread the batter to about ½ in/12 mm from the waffler's edge. Close the lid and bake the waffle to the desired doneness.

Remove the waffle and let it cool for a minute or so on the wire rack before serving. Or set it on the wire rack and slide the baking sheet into the oven to keep the waffle warm. Bake the remaining batter, allowing each waffle to cool a bit before serving, or transferring each one to the rack in the oven.

BELGIAN WAFFLES

Americans tend to call any waffle baked in a Belgian waffle maker (that is, one with extra-large pockets) a Belgian waffle, but a proper Belgian waffle is not only deep-pocketed; it's leavened with yeast instead of baking powder or baking soda. Yeast makes for an extremely light and airy texture, as well as a subtly complex flavor resulting from a gradual rise, or fermentation. In this recipe, the butter that goes into the batter is first browned. If you like, you can opt not to brown the butter, but it's a simple step that produces a deep, rich, nutlike flavor and aroma. Plan ahead when making these waffles so that the batter has at least 12 hours to rise in the refrigerator; the next morning, all you'll have to do is plug in the waffle iron and stir the batter before you're ready to bake. You can, of course, bake these waffles in a regular waffle iron instead of a Belgian waffle iron, but they'll simply be yeasted or raised waffles, rather than true Belgian waffles.

INGREDIENTS

½	cup/115 g unsalted butter
2	cups/480 ml whole milk
2	cups/280 g unbleached all-purpose flour
3	tbsp sugar
1½	tsp instant (rapid-rise) yeast
1	tsp fine sea salt
2	large eggs
1	tsp vanilla extract (optional)

In a medium saucepan, warm the butter over medium-high heat. When it's fully melted, reduce the heat to medium and cook the butter, stirring occasionally, until the milk solids that have collected at the bottom are deeply browned and the butterfat is richly golden, 6 to 8 minutes. Remove the pan from the heat and pour in the milk to halt the cooking. Set the saucepan aside and let the milk mixture cool until just warm to the touch.

In a large bowl, whisk together the flour, sugar, yeast, and salt.

When the milk mixture is just warm, whisk the eggs and vanilla (if using) in a medium bowl. Whisk the milk mixture into the eggs, then pour the liquid ingredients into the dry ingredients and whisk gently just until the batter is evenly moistened. It's fine if some small lumps remain. Give the batter a couple of folds with a rubber spatula to ensure that there aren't any pockets of flour.

Cover the bowl with plastic wrap and refrigerate the batter for at least 12 or up to 24 hours.

When you're ready to make the waffles, if you plan to hold them and serve them all at once rather than one at a time hot off the waffle iron, preheat the oven to 225°F/110°C/gas ¼ and set a large wire rack on a large, rimmed baking sheet.

Preheat a Belgian waffle iron.

Gently stir the batter to deflate it. Pour ½ cup/120 ml of the batter (or the waffler manufacturer's recommended amount) into the center of the waffle iron. Close the lid and bake the waffle to the desired doneness.

CONTINUED >

Remove the waffle and serve it immediately before baking the remaining batter. Or set it on the wire rack and slide the baking sheet into the oven to keep the waffle warm. Bake the remaining batter, transferring each waffle to the rack in the oven.

BELGIAN WAFFLES WITH STRAWBERRIES AND CREAM

This is a typical—and truly delicious—way to enjoy real Belgian waffles. If you like, add other berries to the strawberries after they've macerated, tossing to coat them with the sweetened juices.

For 4 servings, hull and thickly slice 1 lb/455 g strawberries and gently toss them in a medium bowl with 3 to 4 tbsp sugar, depending on their sweetness. Let them stand for about 10 minutes, tossing once or twice, until the sugar dissolves and the berries begin to release their juice. Top each Belgian waffle with a portion of berries and Whipped Cream (page 90) or Sour Cream Whipped Cream (page 80) and serve right away.

HONEYED WHOLE-WHEAT WAFFLES

MAKES ABOUT 8 STANDARD (6½-IN/16.5-CM) ROUND WAFFLES

Heavy, dense, and dry. That's what you're probably thinking. But in fact, these waffles are incredibly light and tender. They'll appeal to even those breakfast-goers like myself who are usually quick to turn down whole-grain baked goods, citing texture as the reason. These waffles also have flavor going for them: browning the butter that goes into the batter creates a rich, hazelnutlike aroma and flavor, and toasting the raw wheat germ brings out its sweet, caramel notes. Together they accentuate the natural nuttiness of the whole-wheat flour. Wheat germ is sold in raw and toasted forms; you can use the latter type instead of toasting your own, but I find the flavor to be superior when freshly toasted.

INGREDIENTS

6	tbsp/85 g unsalted butter
2	cups/480 ml whole milk
2	tbsp honey
¼	cup/20 g raw wheat germ (see recipe introduction)
1	cup/140 g unbleached all-purpose flour
1	cup/140 g whole-wheat flour
2½	tsp baking powder
1	tsp fine sea salt
2	large eggs

In a small saucepan, warm the butter over medium-high heat. When it's fully melted, reduce the heat to medium and cook the butter, stirring occasionally, until the milk solids that have collected at the bottom are deeply browned and the butterfat is richly golden, 6 to 8 minutes. Remove the pan from the heat and pour in the milk to halt the cooking. Add the honey and stir to combine. Set the saucepan aside and let the milk mixture cool until it's barely warm to the touch.

In a medium frying pan, toast the wheat germ over medium heat, stirring frequently, until it is fragrant and the color is a shade or two darker, 8 to 10 minutes. Transfer the toasted wheat germ to a large bowl and let cool slightly. Add both flours, the baking powder, and salt and whisk until well combined.

If you plan to hold the waffles and serve them all at once rather than one at a time hot off the waffle iron, preheat the oven to 225°F/110°C/gas ¼ and set a large wire rack on a large, rimmed baking sheet.

Preheat your waffle iron.

When the milk mixture is just warm, whisk the eggs in a medium bowl. Whisk the milk mixture into the eggs, then pour the liquid ingredients into the dry ingredients and whisk gently just until the batter is evenly moistened. It's fine if some small lumps remain. Give the batter a couple of folds with a rubber spatula to ensure that there aren't any pockets of flour. The batter will be quite fluid.

CONTINUED >

Pour a generous ½ cup/120 ml of the batter (or the waffler manufacturer's recommended amount) into the center of the waffle iron. Close the lid and bake the waffle to the desired doneness.

Remove the waffle and serve it immediately before baking the remaining batter. Or set it on the wire rack and slide the baking sheet into the oven to keep the waffle warm. Bake the remaining batter, transferring each waffle to the rack in the oven.

CHAPTER 2

FRUIT, NUT, AND NOT-SO-PLAIN WAFFLES

Consider, for a moment, waffles as a medium, or as a blank canvas. Include some flavor-packed ingredients in the batter—fruits, nuts, grains, sweeteners, spices, liquids, fats, or, a category unto itself, bacon—and plain waffles take on a very different personality. No longer quiet and demure, they command your ocular or olfactory attention, just before they titillate your palate.

In the next few pages, you'll find such delights as Wild Blueberry–Buttermilk Waffles dotted with lapis-colored fruit and Cornmeal and Bacon Waffles studded with bits of fried bacon; Spicy Pumpkin Waffles of a burnt-orange hue and purplish-gray Buckwheat–Sour Cream Waffles; Pecan–Browned Butter Waffles richly fragrant with toasted nuts and Amber Ale Waffles redolent of yeasty beer. Indeed, any of the waffles in this chapter would add an element of the unexpected to the morning table, transforming any breakfast or brunch into a special meal.

WILD BLUEBERRY-BUTTERMILK WAFFLES

W ild blueberries, which are sold frozen, are tiny and packed full of flavor, making them the best choice for these waffles. Unfortunately, fresh culti-vated blueberries aren't a good substitute for wild berries—they're so big and plump that they won't allow the waffle iron to fully close, which means the batter won't spread and the waffles will bake up too thick and doughy. If cultivated blueberries are your only option and you're jonesing for blueberry waf-fles, consider cooking up a batch of Classic Waffles (page 16), Buttermilk Waffles (page 18), or Golden Cornmeal Waffles (page 20) and serving them with Blueberry Compote (page 94) instead. Top them off with dollops of lightly sweetened sour cream for fla-vor and color contrast. Use the frozen wild berries straight out of the freezer—don't thaw them, but do break them up if they're frozen into large clumps.

INGREDIENTS

2	cups/280 g unbleached all-purpose flour, plus 1 tsp for tossing with the berries
¼	cup/50 g sugar
2	tsp baking powder
¾	tsp fine sea salt
¼	tsp baking soda
2	large eggs
2⅓	cups/555 ml buttermilk, at room temperature
¾	tsp grated lemon zest
½	cup/115 g unsalted butter, melted and cooled slightly
2	cups/280 g frozen wild blueberries

If you plan to hold the waffles and serve them all at once rather than one at a time hot off the waffle iron, preheat the oven to 225°F/110°C/gas ¼ and set a large wire rack on a large, rimmed baking sheet.

Preheat your waffle iron.

In a large bowl, whisk together the 2 cups/280 g flour, sugar, baking powder, salt, and baking soda until well combined.

In a medium bowl, whisk the eggs until combined, and then whisk in the buttermilk and lemon zest. Gradually whisk in the butter.

Pour the liquid ingredients into the dry ingredients, and whisk gently just until the batter is evenly moist-ened. It's fine if some small lumps remain. The batter will be quite thick.

In a medium bowl, toss the frozen blueberries with the 1 tsp flour until the berries are evenly coated; the flour helps minimize the amount that the berries' color will bleed into the batter. Add the berries to the batter, and with a rubber spatula and a few definitive strokes, fold them in; the batter will be streaked with blue.

Pour ½ cup/120 ml of the batter (or the waffler manu-facturer's recommended amount) into the center of the waffle iron. Use the rubber spatula to spread the batter to about ¼ in/6 mm from the waffler's edge. Close the lid and bake the waffle to the desired doneness.

Remove the waffle and serve it immediately before baking the remaining batter. Or set it on the wire rack and slide the baking sheet into the oven to keep the waffle warm. Bake the remaining batter, transferring each waffle to the rack in the oven.

COCONUT² WAFFLES

MAKES ABOUT **7** STANDARD (6½-IN/16.5-CM) ROUND WAFFLES

These über-rich waffles, with a double dose of coconut in the form of unsweetened shreds and milk, will make any coconut lover swoon. Guaranteed. Those who have tasted these waffles agree that there's really nothing that can be put on top that would improve them. But if eating waffles out of hand like a cookie (as coconut waffles are eaten in Vietnam) is too radical, try topping them with sliced bananas and a drizzle of Burnt Caramel Sauce (page 100) or a dollop of Lime Curd Mousseline (page 93). They're on the sweet side, so if you're using them as the waffle base for a dessert (for instance, with vanilla ice cream and Butter-Rum Bananas, page 99), use the smaller amount of sugar. The waffles are floppy straight off the iron, but they crisp as they cool, so be sure to give them a moment of repose before serving.

INGREDIENTS

²/₃	cup/60 g unsweetened shredded coconut, toasted (see page 10)
1¹/₃	cups/180 g unbleached all-purpose flour
4 or 5	tbsp/50 or 60 g sugar
2¼	tsp baking powder
½	tsp fine sea salt
2	large eggs, separated
½	tsp vanilla extract
1¾	cups/420 ml well-stirred coconut milk
3	tbsp/40 g unsalted butter, melted and cooled slightly

If you plan to hold the waffles and serve them all at once rather than one at a time hot off the waffle iron, preheat the oven to 225°F/110°C/gas ¼ and set a large wire rack on a large, rimmed baking sheet.

Preheat your waffle iron.

In a large bowl, whisk together the toasted coconut, flour, sugar, baking powder, and salt until well combined.

In a medium bowl, whisk the egg yolks and vanilla until combined, and then whisk in the coconut milk. Gradually whisk in the butter.

Pour the liquid ingredients into the dry ingredients and whisk gently just until the batter is evenly moistened. It's fine if some small lumps remain. The batter will be quite thick.

In a clean medium bowl, with a clean whisk, rotary beater, or handheld mixer, beat the egg whites until they hold soft peaks. Using a rubber spatula, slide the beaten whites onto the batter and gently fold them in.

Pour ½ cup/120 ml of the batter (or the waffler manufacturer's recommended amount) into the center of the waffle iron. Use the rubber spatula to spread the batter to about ¼ in/6 mm from the waffler's edge. Close the lid and bake the waffle until deep golden brown.

Remove the waffle and let it cool for a minute or so on the wire rack before serving. Or set it on the wire rack and slide the baking sheet into the oven to keep the waffle warm. Bake the remaining batter, allowing each waffle to cool a bit before serving, or transferring each one to the rack in the oven.

SPICY PUMPKIN WAFFLES

MAKES ABOUT **8** **STANDARD (6½-IN/16.5-CM) ROUND WAFFLES**

These waffles are sweet and spicy in the way that pumpkin waffles ought to be, but in addition to the usual warm, aromatic spices, they contain a dose of chipotle powder for piquancy and a scintilla of smokiness. They leave a pleasant tingle on the tongue after the last bite is gone. A generous measure of pumpkin purée gives these soft-crusted waffles a supremely moist, cakelike crumb. I can think of no better accompaniment than butter and warm maple syrup, but Maple Cream Cheese (page 89), with or without a drizzle of Gingery Cranberry-Pineapple Syrup (page 95), would come pretty close.

INGREDIENTS

1¾	cups/250 g unbleached all-purpose flour
2	tsp baking powder
1	tsp fine sea salt
1	tsp ground ginger
1	tsp ground cinnamon
½	tsp chipotle powder
¼	tsp ground nutmeg
	Big pinch of ground cloves
1	cup/240 g pumpkin purée
2	large eggs, separated
3	tbsp packed dark brown sugar
1¼	cups/300 ml whole milk, at room temperature
½	cup/115 g unsalted butter, melted and cooled slightly

If you plan to hold the waffles and serve them all at once rather than one at a time hot off the waffle iron, preheat the oven to 225°F/110°C/gas ¼ and set a large wire rack on a large, rimmed baking sheet.

Preheat your waffle iron.

In a large bowl, whisk together the flour, baking powder, salt, ginger, cinnamon, chipotle powder, nutmeg, and cloves until well combined.

In a medium bowl, whisk together the pumpkin purée, egg yolks, and brown sugar until combined. Add the milk and whisk until the sugar dissolves. Gradually whisk in the butter.

Pour the liquid ingredients into the dry ingredients and whisk gently just until the batter is evenly moistened. It's fine if some small lumps remain.

In a clean medium bowl, with a clean whisk, rotary beater, or handheld mixer, beat the egg whites until they hold soft peaks. Using a rubber spatula, slide the beaten whites onto the batter and gently fold them in. The batter will be quite thick.

Pour a generous ½ cup/120 ml of the batter (or the waffler manufacturer's recommended amount) into the center of the waffle iron. Use the rubber spatula to spread the batter to about ¼ in/6 mm from the waffler's edge. Close the lid and bake the waffle until nicely browned.

Remove the waffle and let it cool for a minute or so on the wire rack before serving. Or set it on the wire rack and slide the baking sheet into the oven to keep the waffle warm. Bake the remaining batter, allowing each waffle to cool a bit before serving, or transferring each one to the rack in the oven.

PEANUT BUTTER WAFFLES

MAKES ABOUT **8** **STANDARD (6½-IN/16.5-CM) ROUND WAFFLES**

If you're a peanut butter fanatic, why put peanut butter *on* your waffle when you can put peanut butter *in* your waffle? That way, your topping options are wide open: maple syrup and honey are good, but so are Maple Cream Cheese (page 89) and Gingery Cranberry-Pineapple Syrup (page 95). Or perhaps a smear of Honey Butter with Orange Essence (page 88) or a drizzle of Bittersweet Chocolate Sauce (page 101). Or more peanut butter, if you must. Be sure to use a natural peanut butter that contains minimal ingredients—preferably only peanuts and salt—so that nothing stands in the way of the true peanut flavor.

INGREDIENTS

1²/₃	cups/235 g unbleached all-purpose flour
1¾	tsp baking powder
¾	tsp fine sea salt
½	tsp baking soda
½	cup/150 g well-stirred natural peanut butter
2	large eggs
2	cups/480 ml buttermilk, at room temperature
2	tbsp packed light brown sugar
2	tbsp unsalted butter, melted and cooled slightly

If you plan to hold the waffles and serve them all at once rather than one at a time hot off the waffle iron, preheat the oven to 225°F/110°C/gas ¼ and set a large wire rack on a large, rimmed baking sheet.

Preheat your waffle iron.

In a large bowl, whisk together the flour, baking powder, salt, and baking soda until well combined.

In a medium bowl, whisk together the peanut butter and the eggs. Add the buttermilk and brown sugar and whisk until the sugar dissolves. Gradually whisk in the butter.

Pour the liquid ingredients into the dry ingredients and whisk gently just until the batter is evenly moistened. It's fine if some small lumps remain. The batter will be quite thick.

Pour a generous ½ cup/120 ml of the batter (or the waffler manufacturer's recommended amount) into the center of the waffle iron. Use a rubber spatula to spread the batter to about ¼ in/6 mm from the waffler's edge. Close the lid and bake the waffle until nicely browned.

Remove the waffle and let it cool for a minute or so on the wire rack before serving. Or set it on the wire rack and slide the baking sheet into the oven to keep the waffle warm. Bake the remaining batter, allowing each waffle to cool a bit before serving, or transferring each one to the rack in the oven.

BANANA-NUT WAFFLES

MAKES ABOUT **9** STANDARD (6½-IN/16.5-CM) ROUND WAFFLES

If you ask me, the best part of a loaf of banana bread is the dark-brown surfaces that form on the top, bottom, and sides—where the sugars caramelize and the flavor is toasty and rich. Enter Banana-Nut Waffles. Baked until they're deeply browned, these waffles are mostly crust surrounding a thin layer of moist, banana-y crumb, so one waffle is like a plateful of prime loaf parts. If you're topping the waffles with a very sweet accompaniment, such as maple syrup, use the smaller amount of sugar; if you're serving them unadorned or with plain butter, use the larger amount.

INGREDIENTS

3	medium-large very ripe bananas (about 18 oz/510 g total weight)
2 or 3	tbsp packed dark brown sugar
2	large eggs
¾	tsp vanilla extract
⅔	cup/165 ml buttermilk, at room temperature
¼	cup/60 ml whole milk, at room temperature
½	cup/115 g unsalted butter, melted and cooled slightly
2	cups/280 g unbleached all-purpose flour
2	tsp baking powder
¾	tsp fine sea salt
¼	tsp baking soda
⅔	cup/75 g finely chopped walnuts or pecans, toasted (see page 10)

Peel the bananas, cut them into rough chunks, and place them in a medium bowl. Add the brown sugar and mash with a dinner fork or potato masher to a thick pulp; small lumps are perfectly fine. Add the eggs and vanilla and whisk well to combine. Whisk in the buttermilk and milk, then gradually whisk in the butter.

If you plan to hold the waffles and serve them all at once rather than one at a time hot off the waffle iron, preheat the oven to 250°F/120°C/gas ½ and set a large wire rack on a large, rimmed baking sheet.

Preheat your waffle iron.

In a large bowl, whisk together the flour, baking powder, salt, and baking soda until well combined. Add the banana mixture and whisk gently just until the batter is evenly moistened. It's fine if some small lumps remain. Gently fold in the nuts with a rubber spatula.

Pour ½ cup/120 ml of the batter (or the waffler manufacturer's recommended amount) into the center of the waffle iron. Use the rubber spatula to spread the batter to about ½ in/12 mm from the waffler's edge. Close the lid and bake the waffle until well browned (these waffles are best when they're deep golden in color).

Remove the waffle and serve it immediately before baking the remaining batter. Or set it on the wire rack and slide the baking sheet into the oven to keep the waffle warm. Bake the remaining batter, transferring each waffle to the rack in the oven.

PECAN-BROWNED BUTTER WAFFLES

MAKES ABOUT **10** STANDARD (6½-IN/16.5-CM) ROUND WAFFLES

It wasn't until I lived in Texas on a street lined with pecan trees and was given a big mesh bag of just-harvested nuts that I began to fully appreciate what pecans have to offer. Fresh out of the shell, they have an amazing butterscotchlike sweetness, the earthiness and warm spice of tobacco, and a subtle smokiness—characteristics that are accentuated with toasting. These waffles are doubly intense with pecans: for flavor, ground nuts are mixed with the flour, and for texture, chopped ones are folded into the batter just before baking. The browned butter magically mimics the pecans' flavor, so the waffles are positively suffused with nutty richness.

INGREDIENTS

½	cup/115 g unsalted butter
1	cup/115 g pecan halves, toasted (see page 10)
1¾	cups/250 g unbleached all-purpose flour
¼	cup/50 g packed dark or light brown sugar
1¾	tsp baking powder
¾	tsp fine sea salt
½	tsp baking soda
⅛	tsp ground cinnamon
2	large eggs, separated
2¼	cups/540 ml buttermilk, at room temperature
½	tsp vanilla extract

In a medium saucepan, warm the butter over medium-high heat. When it's fully melted, reduce the heat to medium and cook the butter, stirring occasionally, until the milk solids that have collected at the bottom are deeply browned and the butterfat is richly golden, 6 to 8 minutes. Pour the browned butter into a small bowl and let cool until just warm.

If you plan to hold the waffles and serve them all at once rather than one at a time hot off the waffle iron, preheat the oven to 225°F/110°C/gas ¼ and set a large wire rack on a large, rimmed baking sheet.

Preheat your waffle iron.

In a food processor, pulse the pecans until very finely chopped, 15 to 18 quick pulses. Remove half of the chopped pecans and set them aside. Add the flour, brown sugar, baking powder, salt, baking soda, and cinnamon to the food processor and process until the nuts are very finely ground, about 20 seconds. Transfer the dry ingredients to a large bowl.

In a medium bowl, whisk together the egg yolks, buttermilk, and vanilla until well combined. Gradually whisk in the browned butter.

Pour the liquid ingredients into the dry ingredients and whisk gently just until the batter is evenly moistened. It's fine if some small lumps remain.

In a clean medium bowl, with a clean whisk, rotary beater, or handheld mixer, beat the egg whites until they hold soft peaks. Using a rubber spatula, slide the beaten whites onto the batter and gently fold them in. The batter will be quite thick.

Pour a generous ½ cup/120 ml of the batter (or the waffler manufacturer's recommended amount) into the center of the waffle iron. Use the rubber spatula to spread the batter to about ¼ in/6 mm from the waffler's edge. Quickly sprinkle a portion (about a scant 1 tbsp of chopped nuts over the batter. Close the lid and bake the waffle until nicely browned.

Remove the waffle and let it cool for a minute or so on the wire rack before serving. Or set it on the wire rack and slide the baking sheet into the oven to keep the waffle warm. Bake the remaining batter, allowing each waffle to cool a bit before serving, or transferring each one to the rack in the oven.

TOASTED OATMEAL WAFFLES WITH A HINT OF CINNAMON

MAKES ABOUT 9 STANDARD (6½-IN/16.5-CM) ROUND WAFFLES

The cooked oatmeal that goes into this batter starts with quick-cooking rolled oats (don't use old-fashioned or instant!) that are toasted in a bit of butter until they give off an amazing aroma. Toasting is an extra step, but it's well worth the effort for the alluring, butterscotchy quality that it brings out in the grain. Be sure to add the buttermilk to the oatmeal while the cereal is still quite warm, before it begins to set up into a starchy mass. As for cooking, bake the waffles until they're deeply browned so that they form a delicately crisp crust that contrasts beautifully with the moist, custardy interior.

INGREDIENTS

6	tbsp/85 g unsalted butter
1	cup/100 g quick-cooking rolled oats
1¾	cups/420 ml water
2	tbsp packed light or dark brown sugar
1	cup/240 ml buttermilk
1	cup/140 g unbleached all-purpose flour
1¾	tsp baking powder
¾	tsp fine sea salt
¼	tsp ground cinnamon
¼	tsp baking soda
2	large eggs, beaten

Melt 1 tbsp of the butter in a large saucepan over medium heat. Add the oats and cook, stirring frequently, until they're browned and smell deeply rich and toasty, 8 to 10 minutes. Remove the saucepan from the heat and carefully pour in the water; the water will steam and sputter, so use caution. Bring the mixture to a boil over high heat, and then turn down the heat to maintain a simmer; the oatmeal should smell remarkable, with an aroma of freshly ground peanut butter. Cook, stirring occasionally, until the oats have absorbed the water and the oatmeal is thick and creamy, about 3 minutes. Transfer to a medium bowl, add the remaining 5 tbsp butter and the brown sugar, and stir until fully incorporated. Stir in the buttermilk. Set the mixture aside to cool slightly, about 10 minutes.

If you plan to hold the waffles and serve them all at once rather than one at a time hot off the waffle iron, preheat the oven to 225°F/110°C/gas ¼ and set a large wire rack on a large, rimmed baking sheet.

Preheat your waffle iron.

In a large bowl, whisk together the flour, baking powder, salt, cinnamon, and baking soda until well combined.

Whisk the beaten eggs into the oatmeal mixture.

Pour the oatmeal mixture into the dry ingredients and fold gently with a rubber spatula just until the batter is evenly moistened.

CONTINUED >

Pour a generous ½ cup/120 ml of the batter (or the waffler manufacturer's recommended amount) into the center of the waffle iron. Use the rubber spatula to spread the batter to about ½ in/12 mm from the waffler's edge. Close the lid and bake the waffle to the desired doneness.

Remove the waffle and serve it immediately before baking the remaining batter. Or set it on the wire rack and slide the baking sheet into the oven to keep the waffle warm. Bake the remaining batter, transferring each waffle to the rack in the oven.

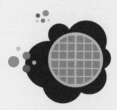

BUCKWHEAT-SOUR CREAM WAFFLES

MAKES ABOUT **8** **STANDARD (6½-IN/16.5-CM) ROUND WAFFLES**

Buckwheat waffles are the lesser-known cousins of Russian buckwheat blini and French buckwheat crêpes (called *galettes*, for some reason). Thanks to the buckwheat flour, everything about these waffles is muscular—from the resilient, elastic consistency of the batter to the waffles' striking speckled gray-purple appearance, earthy roasted flavor with notes of smokiness, and sturdy structure. Quite surprisingly, these waffles with so much character are extremely versatile—they're equally good doused with maple syrup or served beneath smoked salmon (see page 60), topped with sautéed apples (see page 98) and spoonfuls of crème fraîche, or simply finished with orange-flavored butter (see page 88).

INGREDIENTS

1	cup/140 g unbleached all-purpose flour
1	cup/140 g buckwheat flour
2	tsp baking powder
¾	tsp fine sea salt
¼	tsp baking soda
2	large eggs
1	cup/240 ml sour cream, at room temperature
1	cup/240 ml whole milk, at room temperature
1½	tbsp packed light or dark brown sugar
½	cup/115 g unsalted butter, melted and cooled slightly

If you plan to hold the waffles and serve them all at once rather than one at a time hot off the waffle iron, preheat the oven to 225°F/110°C/gas ¼ and set a large wire rack on a large, rimmed baking sheet.

Preheat your waffle iron.

In a large bowl, whisk together both flours, the baking powder, salt, and baking soda until well combined.

In a medium bowl, whisk the eggs until combined, and then whisk in the sour cream, milk, and brown sugar and mix until the sugar dissolves. Gradually whisk in the butter.

Pour the liquid ingredients into the dry ingredients and whisk gently just until the batter is evenly moistened. It will be quite thick and almost gluey because of the buckwheat. Give the batter a couple of folds with a rubber spatula to ensure that there aren't any pockets of flour.

Pour a generous ½ cup/120 ml of the batter (or the waffler manufacturer's recommended amount) into the center of the waffle iron. Use the rubber spatula to spread the batter to about ½ in/12 mm from the waffler's edge. Close the lid and bake the waffle to the desired doneness.

Remove the waffle and serve it immediately before baking the remaining batter. Or set it on the wire rack and slide the baking sheet into the oven to keep the waffle warm. Bake the remaining batter, transferring each waffle to the rack in the oven.

ANADAMA WAFFLES WITH CURRANTS

MAKES ABOUT **8** STANDARD (6½-IN/16.5-CM) ROUND WAFFLES

This recipe is modeled after anadama bread, an old-time New England bread containing cornmeal and molasses. The story goes that a farmer or fisherman (depending on who's telling the story) was tired of the cornmeal and molasses gruel that his wife served him for breakfast day in and day out. Exasperated and muttering "Anna, damn her," he mixed some flour and yeast into his porridge and baked the mixture, thereby creating the very first loaf of anadama bread. Dark molasses gives these waffles the best flavor and color; if you have light molasses on hand, up the amount to 3 tbsp. Whatever you do, don't use blackstrap molasses, which is far too potent for this recipe. The batter must rise in the refrigerator for up to 24 hours before baking, so plan accordingly.

INGREDIENTS

1¼	cups/175 g unbleached all-purpose flour
1	cup/150 g fine stone-ground (whole-grain) yellow cornmeal
1½	tsp instant (rapid-rise) yeast
1	tsp fine sea salt
2	large eggs
1¾	cups/420 ml whole milk
½	cup/115 g unsalted butter, melted and cooled slightly
2	tbsp dark molasses (see recipe introduction)
2½	tbsp packed dark brown sugar
½	cup/70 g currants

In a large bowl, whisk together the flour, cornmeal, yeast, and salt.

Whisk the eggs in a medium bowl, then whisk in the milk, followed by the butter. Add the molasses and brown sugar and whisk until the sugar dissolves. Pour the liquid ingredients into the dry ingredients and whisk gently just until the batter is evenly moistened. It's fine if some small lumps remain. Give the batter a couple of folds with a rubber spatula to ensure that there aren't any pockets of flour.

Cover the bowl with plastic wrap and refrigerate the batter for at least 12 or up to 24 hours.

When you're ready to make waffles, if you plan to hold the waffles and serve them all at once rather than one at a time hot off the waffle iron, preheat the oven to 225°F/110°C/gas ¼ and set a large wire rack on a large, rimmed baking sheet.

Preheat your waffle iron.

Stir the batter to deflate it and to incorporate any liquid that has settled on the bottom. Gently fold in the currants. Pour ½ cup/120 ml of the batter (or the waffler manufacturer's recommended amount) into the center of the waffle iron. Close the lid and bake the waffle to the desired doneness.

Remove the waffle and serve it immediately before baking the remaining batter. Or set it on the wire rack and slide the baking sheet into the oven to keep it warm; bake the remaining batter, transferring each waffle to the rack in the oven.

CORNMEAL AND BACON WAFFLES

MAKES ABOUT **8** **STANDARD (6½-IN/16.5-CM) ROUND WAFFLES**

At the breakfast table, if I've got a waffle in front of me, chances are good that there's bacon on the periphery. These waffles, then, are about efficiency, because the bacon is *in* the waffle. They're also about being tasty—bacon fat goes into the waffle batter, so there's a good dose of smoke and salt to balance the sweetness of the maple syrup that you've surely poured over the waffles. But these are not only for mornings. Cornmeal and Bacon Waffles are perfect for accompanying a bowl of chowder or chili and can stand in for cornbread at just about any time.

INGREDIENTS

8	oz/225 g bacon, chopped into ½-in/12-mm pieces
3	tbsp/40 g unsalted butter, cut into pieces
1	cup/140 g unbleached all-purpose flour
1	cup/150 g fine stone-ground (whole-grain) yellow cornmeal
1	tbsp sugar
1¾	tsp baking powder
¾	tsp fine sea salt
¼	tsp baking soda
¼	tsp freshly ground black pepper
2	large eggs
2	cups/480 ml buttermilk, at room temperature

In a medium frying pan over medium-high heat, cook the bacon, stirring frequently, until browned and crisped, 8 to 10 minutes. Using a slotted spoon, transfer the bacon to a plate lined with paper towels.

Measure out 3 tbsp bacon fat into a small bowl; add the butter and allow it to melt with the residual heat of the bacon fat.

If you plan to hold the waffles and serve them all at once rather than one at a time hot off the waffle iron, preheat the oven to 225°F/110°C/gas ¼ and set a large wire rack on a large, rimmed baking sheet.

Preheat your waffle iron.

In a large bowl, whisk together the flour, cornmeal, sugar, baking powder, salt, baking soda, and pepper until well combined.

In a medium bowl, whisk the eggs until combined, and then whisk in the buttermilk. Gradually whisk in the bacon fat–butter mixture.

Pour the liquid ingredients into the dry ingredients and whisk gently just until the batter is evenly moistened. Sprinkle the bacon pieces over the batter and gently fold them in until evenly distributed.

Pour a generous ½ cup/120 ml of the batter (or the waffler manufacturer's recommended amount) into the center of the waffle iron. Use a rubber spatula to spread the batter to about ½ in/12 mm from the waffler's edge. Close the lid and bake the waffle to the desired doneness.

Remove the waffle and let it cool for a minute or so on the wire rack before serving. Or set it on the wire rack and slide the baking sheet into the oven to keep the waffle warm. Bake the remaining batter, allowing each waffle to cool a bit before serving, or transferring each one to the rack in the oven.

AMBER ALE WAFFLES

MAKES ABOUT **8** STANDARD (6½-IN/16.5-CM) ROUND WAFFLES

Beer waffles? Indeed! Choose a bold, assertive amber ale to use in these waffles. It'll give them a deep, roasted, hoppy flavor with just enough bitter bite to let you know that it's in there. And with notes of warm spices, molasses, and yeast—and smokiness from maple syrup, if that's your accompaniment of choice—the flavors here are so intriguing that it's hard to put the fork down when you've got a plate of these in front of you. You could substitute a lighter beer, like a lager or pilsner, but that would be missing the point of making these waffles in the first place. They're also great used as savories—my friend Adam, who tested this recipe, can vouch for their fabulousness as the "bread" in a turkey and Swiss cheese sandwich.

INGREDIENTS	
2	cups/280 g unbleached all-purpose flour
2¼	tsp baking powder
¾	tsp fine sea salt
¼	tsp ground nutmeg
2	large eggs
One	12-oz/360-ml bottle full-bodied amber ale
¼	cup/60 ml whole milk
2½	tbsp packed dark or light brown sugar
6	tbsp/85 g unsalted butter, melted and cooled slightly

If you plan to hold the waffles and serve them all at once rather than one at a time hot off the waffle iron, preheat the oven to 225°F/110°C/gas ¼ and set a large wire rack on a large, rimmed baking sheet.

Preheat your waffle iron.

In a large bowl, whisk together the flour, baking powder, salt, and nutmeg until well combined.

In a medium bowl, whisk the eggs until combined, and then whisk in the ale, milk, and brown sugar and mix until the sugar dissolves. Gradually whisk in the butter.

Pour the liquid ingredients into the dry ingredients and whisk gently just until the batter is evenly moistened. Give the batter a couple of folds with a rubber spatula to ensure that there aren't any pockets of flour. The batter will be quite fluid.

Pour ½ cup/120 ml of the batter (or the waffler manufacturer's recommended amount) into the center of the waffle iron. Use the rubber spatula to even it out and distribute it slightly (but there's no need to spread it all the way to the edges). Close the lid and bake the waffle to the desired doneness.

Remove the waffle and serve it immediately before baking the remaining batter. Or set it on the wire rack and slide the baking sheet into the oven to keep it warm; bake the remaining batter, transferring each waffle to the rack in the oven.

VARIATION

AMBER ALE WAFFLES WITH BACON

Beer and bacon waffles, topped with butter and doused with maple syrup, sound gluttonous—and I suppose they are—but taste astonishingly good.

Chop 8 oz/225 g bacon into ½-in/12-mm pieces. In a medium frying pan over medium-high heat, cook the bacon, stirring frequently, until browned and crisped, 8 to 10 minutes. Using a slotted spoon, transfer the bacon to a plate lined with paper towels. Make Amber Ale Waffles, sprinkling about 1 tbsp of the fried bacon over the batter that's been poured into the waffle iron, before closing the lid. Bake as usual.

CHAPTER 3
SAVORIES

In casual conversation, the mention of nonsweet waffles always raises a few quizzical eyebrows. After a moment of consideration, though, it all makes sense—change up the ingredients a bit and a waffle can stand in for the carbohydrate component in a number of different dishes. Take, for example, waffles as crackers in Mini Salt-and-Pepper Waffles with Bacon–Green Onion Clam Dip, as bread in Ham and Gruyère Waffle Tartines, as biscuits in Waffles with Sausage Gravy, or as tortillas in Huevos y Waffles Rancheros. Waffles, by adding an element of the unexpected, make these renditions delightful and whimsical. But a savory waffle can be good in its own right, too. Add cheese and herbs to the batter and the results are waffles so tasty that they're fluently savory.

Perhaps the most well-known, well-loved waffle in the savory family—and the granddaddy to them all—is waffles with fried chicken. In this dish, purportedly Southern in origin, waffles retain their own identity and, oftentimes, maple syrup as a partner! It's seemingly a mismatch, but the very tasty duo of waffles and fried poultry has even inspired a spate of upscale restaurant dishes. Chicken-fried foie gras on waffles, anyone? Not for me, thanks. I'll stick with Fried Chicken and Waffles with Bacon Gravy. Some foods aren't comfortable going uptown.

MINI SALT-AND-PEPPER WAFFLES WITH BACON-GREEN ONION CLAM DIP

MAKES ABOUT MINI (2- TO 2½-IN/16.5-CM) WAFFLES

Okay, so the "dip" here isn't really a dip because each mini waffle is topped with a spoonful before serving. But if you so desired, you could serve the mini waffles unadorned, for actual dipping. If you go that route, consider doubling the dip because it's highly addictive, and with dippers left to their own devices, the bowl may empty out very quickly. You don't need any special equipment to make mini waffles. By spooning small dollops of batter onto the center of each section that makes up the waffle-iron grid, you can make several minis at once. (For example, a standard round iron that makes a four-section waffle will yield four mini waffles.) A standard waffle iron works much better for this purpose than a Belgian or heart-shaped waffler.

INGREDIENTS

DIP

4	oz/115 g bacon
One	6½-oz/185-g can chopped clams, drained well
6	tbsp/90 ml mayonnaise
6	tbsp/90 ml sour cream
2	green onions, thinly sliced
1	tsp fresh lemon juice
½	tsp Worcestershire sauce
⅛	tsp ground celery seed
	Fine sea salt and freshly ground black pepper

MINI WAFFLES

1	cup/140 g unbleached all-purpose flour
2	tsp sugar
1¼	tsp baking powder
½	tsp fine sea salt
½	tsp freshly ground black pepper
1	large egg
1	cup/240 ml whole milk, at room temperature
3	tbsp/40 g unsalted butter, melted and cooled slightly
	Freshly ground black pepper
1 or 2	green onions, green parts only, thinly sliced on the diagonal

CONTINUED >

TO MAKE THE DIP: In a medium frying pan over medium-high heat, cook the bacon, stirring frequently, until browned and crisped, 8 to 10 minutes. Using a slotted spoon, transfer the bacon to a plate lined with paper towels and set aside to cool.

In a small bowl, combine the clams, mayonnaise, sour cream, green onions, lemon juice, Worcestershire sauce, celery seed, and bacon and stir until well blended. Season with salt and pepper. Cover with plastic wrap and refrigerate for at least 1 hour or up to 24 hours to allow the flavors to meld.

TO MAKE THE WAFFLES: In a medium bowl, whisk together the flour, sugar, baking powder, salt, and pepper until well combined.

In a small bowl, whisk the egg until combined, and then whisk in the milk. Gradually whisk in the butter.

Pour the liquid ingredients into the dry ingredients and whisk gently just until the batter is evenly moistened. Give the batter a couple of folds with a rubber spatula to ensure that there aren't any pockets of flour. The batter will be quite fluid. Let the batter stand for about 5 minutes; it will thicken slightly.

Meanwhile, set a large wire rack on a large, rimmed baking sheet. Preheat a standard (not Belgian) waffle iron.

Using a 1-tbsp measuring spoon and working quickly, pour about 2 tsp batter into the center of each quadrant, rectangle, or square that makes up the larger grid—the amount of batter will seem extremely scant. Close the lid and bake the waffles until well browned and crisp. It may take a couple of rounds to get the size of the mini waffles just right. Transfer the waffles to the wire rack and repeat with the remaining batter. You should have about 45 mini waffles—more than you'll need—but the remainder freezes well.

Spoon about 2 tsp dip onto each mini waffle. Sprinkle with pepper and garnish with a few slices of green onion. Arrange the mini waffles on a platter or tray and serve right away.

FINES HERBES AND EMMENTALER WAFFLES

MAKES STANDARD (6½-IN/16.5-CM) ROUND WAFFLES

In classic French cooking, *fines herbes* are a mélange of delicate fresh herbs that always includes chives, chervil, and tarragon, and sometimes a few others. The blend is highly aromatic but not overpowering. The abundance of fines herbes in the batter gives these waffles a short shelf life (meaning that they don't freeze very well), which is why this recipe makes only four standard waffles. However, if you require more servings, the recipe can easily be doubled. A poached egg is the perfect accoutrement for each one of these waffles; when broken into, the yolk creates a luscious sauce. And a side of crisp fried bacon wouldn't be too shabby, either.

INGREDIENTS

1	cup/140 g unbleached all-purpose flour
1	tsp baking powder
½	tsp fine sea salt
¼	tsp freshly ground black pepper
¼	tsp sugar
2	oz/55 g Emmentaler cheese, shredded
1	large egg
1	cup/240 ml whole milk, at room temperature
3	tbsp unsalted butter, melted and cooled slightly
1½	tbsp minced fresh chives
1½	tbsp minced fresh chervil and tarragon (in the proportion of your preference)

If you plan to hold the waffles and serve them all at once rather than one at a time hot off the waffle iron, preheat the oven to 225°F/110°C/gas ¼ and set a large wire rack on a large, rimmed baking sheet.

Preheat your waffle iron.

In a medium bowl, whisk together the flour, baking powder, salt, pepper, and sugar until well combined. Add the cheese and toss to combine, breaking up any clumps.

In a small bowl, whisk the egg until combined, and then whisk in the milk. Gradually whisk in the butter.

Pour the liquid ingredients into the dry ingredients and whisk gently just until the batter is evenly moistened. Add the herbs and fold them into the batter with a rubber spatula until they're evenly distributed.

Pour ½ cup/120 ml of the batter (or the waffler manufacturer's recommended amount) into the center of the waffle iron. Use the rubber spatula to spread the batter to about ½ in/12 mm from the waffler's edge. Close the lid and bake the waffle until deep golden brown.

Remove the waffle and serve it immediately before baking the remaining batter. Or set it on the wire rack and slide the baking sheet into the oven to keep it warm; bake the remaining batter, transferring each waffle to the rack in the oven.

CORNMEAL WAFFLES WITH CHEDDAR, CHIPOTLE CHILE, AND GREEN ONIONS

MAKES ABOUT STANDARD (6½-IN/16.5-CM) ROUND WAFFLES

Some ingredients are just meant to be together, and I think the ones in this recipe are prime examples. So when I thought up these waffles, I figured they'd taste good, but to be honest, I hadn't an inkling how outstandingly yummy they'd be. With crisp surfaces and patches of browned cheese, a delicate interior crunch from the cornmeal, and a savory-sweet-spicy-smoky-sharp flavor through and through, these waffles are bona fide winners. Serve them for breakfast with eggs or as an accompaniment to a big pot of chili. Or just eat them hot off the waffle iron.

INGREDIENTS

1	cup/140 g unbleached all-purpose flour
1	cup/150 g fine stone-ground (whole-grain) yellow cornmeal
1	tbsp sugar
2	tsp baking powder
½	tsp fine sea salt
¼	tsp baking soda
4	oz/115 g sharp Cheddar cheese, shredded
2	large eggs
1¾	cups/420 ml buttermilk
1	tbsp minced seeded chipotle chile in adobo
6	tbsp/85 g unsalted butter, melted and cooled slightly
3 or 4	green onions, thinly sliced

If you plan to hold the waffles and serve them all at once rather than one at a time hot off the waffle iron, preheat the oven to 225°F/110°C/gas ¼ and set a large wire rack on a large, rimmed baking sheet.

Preheat your waffle iron.

In a large bowl, whisk together the flour, cornmeal, sugar, baking powder, salt, and baking soda until well combined. Add the cheese and toss to combine, breaking up any clumps.

In a medium bowl, whisk the eggs until combined, and then whisk in the buttermilk and chipotle chile. Gradually whisk in the butter.

Pour the liquid ingredients into the dry ingredients and whisk gently just until the batter is evenly moistened. Add the green onions and fold them into the batter with a rubber spatula until they're evenly distributed. The batter will be quite thick.

Pour a generous ½ cup/120 ml of the batter (or the waffler manufacturer's recommended amount) into the center of the waffle iron. Use the rubber spatula to spread the batter to about ½ in/12 mm from the waffler's edge. Close the lid and bake the waffle until deep golden brown.

Remove the waffle and serve it immediately before baking the remaining batter. Or set it on the wire rack and slide the baking sheet into the oven to keep it warm; bake the remaining batter, transferring each waffle to the rack in the oven.

HAM AND GRUYÈRE WAFFLE TARTINES

MAKES SERVINGS

A *tartine* can be a slice of bread simply topped with butter and preserves, or it can be a more elaborate open-faced sandwich. (Leave it to the French to give even the humblest foods such a charming name.) This recipe employs waffles as the bread and combines the free-spirited toplessness of a *tartine* sandwich with classic *croque monsieur* ingredients. Waffle *tartines* make a satisfying breakfast or, with a vinaigrette-dressed salad served alongside, an excellent midday meal or light dinner. If you've got Classic Waffles in your freezer and are looking for an out-of-the-ordinary way to use them, here's your answer.

INGREDIENTS

MORNAY SAUCE

2	tbsp unsalted butter
2	tbsp unbleached all-purpose flour
1	cup/240 ml whole milk
½	cup/55 g shredded Gruyère cheese
	Pinch of ground nutmeg
	Pinch of cayenne
	Fine sea salt and freshly ground black pepper
4	standard Classic Waffles (page 16)
12	oz/340 g good-quality sliced ham
¾	cup/85 g shredded Gruyère cheese
	Whole-grain mustard, for serving
	Cornichons, for serving

Preheat the oven to 500°F/260°C/gas 10. Line a rimmed baking sheet with aluminim foil.

TO MAKE THE SAUCE: In a small saucepan over medium heat, melt the butter. Whisk in the flour to make a roux and cook for about 2 minutes. Whisking constantly, gradually pour in the milk. Once all the milk is in, increase the heat to medium-high and bring the mixture to a boil. Reduce the heat to maintain a steady but not overly vigorous simmer and cook the sauce, whisking occasionally, until it is nicely thickened and the starchy taste of the flour has been cooked out, about 5 minutes. Remove the pan from the heat, add the cheese, and whisk until the cheese is melted and the sauce is smooth. Whisk in the nutmeg and cayenne, and then season with salt and pepper. Set the sauce aside.

Lay out the waffles on the prepared baking sheet. Top each waffle with a portion of ham. Spoon one-quarter of the sauce over the ham on each waffle and spread the sauce to about ½ in/12 mm of the edge. Sprinkle shredded Gruyère on each, dividing it evenly. Bake until the cheese is melted and spotty brown, 8 to 10 minutes. (If the cheese is not yet browned, turn on the broiler and broil the tartines until the cheese begins to color; this should take no longer than a minute.)

Let the tartines cool for a few minutes, then transfer them to individual plates. Serve right away, passing whole-grain mustard and cornichons at the table.

HUEVOS Y WAFFLES RANCHEROS

MAKES SERVINGS

During the time we lived in Texas, huevos rancheros were a frequent Sunday breakfast. My other half finds this gringo version of the dish—in which cornmeal waffles replace the corn tortillas on which the fried eggs rest—an improvement over traditional huevos rancheros, the reason being that a waffle has more presence than a tortilla. A waffle is also absorbent, so it takes in the runny egg yolk and ranchero sauce, making each forkful a complete one. A smear of doctored-up refried beans on top of the waffle, before the egg is put in place, is a mucho tasty addition, but you can skip the beans and the results will still taste great.

INGREDIENTS

RANCHERO SAUCE

1½	lb/680 g ripe plum tomatoes, cored
1	jalapeño chile
½	cup/55 g coarsely chopped white onion
2	garlic cloves, coarsely chopped
2	tbsp vegetable or olive oil
	Fine sea salt and freshly ground black pepper

REFRIED BEANS

2	oz/55 g bacon, finely chopped
	Vegetable or olive oil, if needed
⅓	cup/40 g finely chopped white onion
One	15-oz/425-g can refried beans
2 to 3	tbsp water
	Fresh lime juice
	Fine sea salt and freshly ground black pepper

FRIED EGGS

	Nonstick cooking spray or 1 tbsp vegetable or olive oil
4	large eggs
	Fine sea salt and freshly ground black pepper

4	standard Golden Cornmeal Waffles (page 20), Cornmeal and Bacon Waffles (page 45), or Cornmeal Waffles with Cheddar, Chipotle Chile, and Green Onions (page 54), recrisped and warm (see Reviving Your Waffles, page 13)

TO MAKE THE SAUCE: Position an oven rack about 4 in/10 cm from the upper heating element and preheat the broiler. Arrange the tomatoes and jalapeño on a rimmed baking sheet and broil, turning as needed, until the skins are well charred, about 12 minutes. Some tomatoes may be done sooner than others; as they're ready, transfer them to a blender jar. When the jalapeño is ready, set it on a cutting board. Trim off the stem end of the jalapeño and peel off the blackened skin. Cut the chile in half lengthwise. If you're wary of spiciness, remove the seeds and ribs, and then add the pod to the blender jar with the tomatoes; if you welcome chile heat, just throw both halves, with seeds and ribs, in the blender. Add the onion and garlic to the blender and purée until smooth.

Heat the oil in a medium saucepan over medium-high heat until shimmering. Add the purée and ½ tsp salt and bring to a vigorous simmer. Turn down the heat to maintain a gentle simmer and cook, stirring occasionally, until the onion and garlic have lost their raw edge and the sauce is slightly thickened, 8 to 10 minutes. Taste the sauce and adjust the seasoning with salt and pepper. Cover to keep warm. (The sauce will keep in an airtight container in the refrigerator for up to 1 week; reheat before using.)

TO MAKE THE BEANS: In a medium saucepan over medium-high heat, fry the bacon until it is lightly browned and the fat has rendered, about 5 minutes.

If there appears to be less than 1 tbsp of fat in the pan, supplement with some oil; if there's more, leave it in the pan. Add the onion, turn down the heat to medium-low, and cook until the onion is softened but not browned, about 5 minutes. Add the beans and the water and stir until the mixture is well combined and the beans are creamy in texture. Cook, stirring frequently, until the beans are heated through and the flavors have melded, about 4 minutes. Season with lime juice, salt, and pepper. Cover to keep warm.

TO MAKE THE EGGS: Heat a large, nonstick frying pan over medium heat until hot. Coat the inside of the pan with nonstick cooking spray or add the oil and swirl to coat. Crack the eggs into the pan and sprinkle with salt and pepper. Cover and cook until the whites are set but the yolks are still runny, about 2 minutes.

Spread some beans on each waffle. (You'll have some left over; they'll keep in an airtight container in the refrigerator for up to 1 week.) Set the waffles on individual plates and top each with a fried egg. Spoon ranchero sauce over each portion and serve right away.

SMOKED SALMON AND CRÈME FRAÎCHE ON BUCKWHEAT-SOUR CREAM WAFFLES

MAKES **6** TO **8** SERVINGS

In these elegant little assemblages that are a classic combination of ingredients, buckwheat waffles stand in for blini. Crème fraîche is luxe in both taste and texture; I think it brings an extra layer of opulence to the dish, but you can use sour cream if you'd prefer a brighter, tangier flavor. Serve the waffles as part of a brunch or light lunch, or as a first course or an *amuse-bouche* in a continental-style dinner.

Cut the waffles into sections and set the pieces on a platter or on individual plates.

Arrange a portion of salmon on each piece and spoon a dollop of crème fraîche on top of the salmon. Lay a few slices of red onion on top of the crème fraîche and sprinkle with chives, followed by capers. Finally, sprinkle sea salt over the top and finish with a light grinding of black pepper. Serve right away.

INGREDIENTS

3 or 4	standard Buckwheat-Sour Cream Waffles (page 43), recrisped and warm (see Reviving Your Waffles, page 13)
8	oz/225 g smoked salmon
½	cup/120 ml crème fraîche
	Very thinly sliced red onion
	Minced fresh chives or chopped fresh dill
2	tbsp nonpareil capers, rinsed and drained
	Flaky sea salt
	Freshly ground black pepper

FRIED CHICKEN AND WAFFLES
WITH BACON GRAVY

MAKES SERVINGS

There's no arguing that fried chicken and waffles are a curious combination, but this unlikely marriage is popular for a reason: it's wonderfully unapologetic. Whatever its roots may be—and they are unclear—it's now an I-want-it-all dish that puts sweet with savory, breakfast with dinner, finger food with fork-and-knife necessity. In a good version of chicken and waffles, the ratio of crust-and-crunch to interior is about as high as it gets for a main dish (matched, perhaps, only by fish and chips), so it appeals to those of us who like a lot of texture on our plate. Traditionally, chicken and waffles is a breakfast dish, but I'm willing to bet that in most households, frying is more likely to happen in the evening than in the morning. With that in mind, this recipe includes gravy—albeit bacon gravy—as an alternative to the usual maple syrup that's offered for dousing the waffle. But if you want it all, you can, of course, serve up both. Plan ahead when making this recipe, because the chicken must brine for 12 to 24 hours.

INGREDIENTS

1	whole chicken (3 to 3½ lb/1.4 to 1.6 kg)

BUTTERMILK BRINE

2½	cups/600 ml buttermilk
3	large garlic cloves, crushed and peeled
1	bay leaf, crumbled
1	tbsp fine sea salt
½	tsp paprika

DREDGING AND FRYING

2½	cups/355 g unbleached all-purpose flour
1½	tsp fine sea salt
1	tsp freshly ground black pepper
1½	cups/360 ml buttermilk
3	cups/720 ml peanut oil or vegetable oil, plus more as needed

GRAVY

6	oz/170 g bacon, finely chopped
2	tbsp unbleached all-purpose flour
2½	cups/540 ml whole milk
1	small bay leaf
	Few dashes hot sauce, such as Tabasco
	Fine sea salt and freshly ground black pepper
4	standard Classic Waffles (page 16), Malted Waffles (page 19), Buttermilk Waffles (page 18), or Golden Cornmeal Waffles (page 20), recrisped and warm (see Reviving Your Waffles, page 13)

CONTINUED >

Cut the chicken into ten serving pieces: 2 thighs, 2 drumsticks, 4 breast pieces (cut each breast half crosswise into two pieces), and 2 wing sections with wing tips removed (save the wings for another meal if desired). Discard the back or reserve for making stock.

TO MAKE THE BRINE: In a large, nonreactive bowl, stir together the buttermilk, garlic, bay leaf, salt, and paprika until the salt dissolves. Submerge the chicken pieces in the brine, cover, and refrigerate for at least 12 hours or up to 24 hours.

Drain the chicken pieces in a large colander, shaking the colander to remove excess buttermilk. If any pieces of garlic or bay leaf are clinging to the chicken, pick them off.

TO DREDGE AND FRY: Set two wire racks over rimmed baking sheets. In a large, shallow baking dish, stir together the flour, salt, and pepper. Pour the buttermilk into a smaller shallow baking dish.

Working with two pieces at a time, dredge the chicken pieces in the flour until coated on all sides. Shake off the excess flour and set each piece on one of the wire racks. (You'll use the other rack to keep the cooked chicken warm.) Once all the pieces have been dredged, give them a double coating: one at a time, dip the pieces into the buttermilk, coating them on all sides. Let the excess drip off, and then dredge the pieces in the flour. Shake off the excess

flour and return the chicken to the wire rack. Let the chicken dry at room temperature for 30 to 45 minutes.

Position one oven rack in the upper third of the oven and preheat the oven to 200°F/95°C/gas ¼.

Pour oil into a 12-in/30.5-cm straight-sided frying pan, preferably cast iron, to a depth of about ½ in/12 mm. Heat the oil over medium-high heat until it reaches about 365°F/180°C.

Add half of the chicken pieces, skin-side down, cover the pan partway, and fry until the bottoms are dark golden brown, 12 to 15 minutes, using tongs to check on the pieces from time to time. Adjust the heat as needed to keep the oil between 300°F/150°C and 325°F/165°C. Turn the pieces and fry the second sides, uncovered this time, until dark golden brown, 10 to 12 minutes. Transfer the chicken to the clean wire rack and slide the baking sheet onto the upper rack in the oven. Bring the oil back up to 365°F/180°C, and then fry the second batch of chicken in the same manner. Transfer the pieces to the rack in the oven to keep the chicken warm.

TO MAKE THE GRAVY: Set a fine-mesh strainer over a heatproof bowl. Strain the frying fat into the bowl, and reserve the drippings in the strainer. Add the bacon to the now-empty frying pan and cook over medium-high heat until browned and crisp, 8 to 10 minutes. Using a slotted spoon, transfer the bacon to a plate, leaving the fat behind.

Pour off all but 2 tbsp fat from the frying pan; if you happen to have less than 2 tbsp fat, make up the difference with some of the strained frying fat. Whisk the flour into the fat in the pan to make a roux and cook over medium heat for about 2 minutes. Whisking constantly, gradually pour in the milk. Once all the milk is in, add the bay leaf, increase the heat to medium-high, and bring the mixture to a boil. Reduce the heat to maintain a steady but not overly vigorous simmer and cook the gravy, whisking occasionally, until it is nicely thickened and the starchy taste of the flour has been cooked out, 5 to 6 minutes.

Return the bacon to the frying pan along with the drippings in the strainer and continue to simmer to bring the flavors together, about 3 minutes. Stir in the hot sauce, and then season the gravy with salt and pepper. Transfer the gravy to a gravy boat or serving bowl.

Set a warm waffle on each plate. Top each waffle with two pieces of chicken. Serve right away, passing the gravy at the table.

WAFFLES WITH SAUSAGE GRAVY

MAKES **4** SERVINGS

Biscuits smothered in sausage gravy (a.k.a. country gravy) are a Southern breakfast tradition, but frankly I think waffles have it all over biscuits in this dish, because a waffle has more crust and less crumb, and so it holds up nicely under gravy rather than being bedraggled by it. This comfort food is super hearty and extremely rich, but so outrageously tasty that it's all too easy to polish off a serving. To gild the lily or really fuel up for the day, top each serving with a runny-yolk fried egg.

INGREDIENTS

GRAVY

12	oz/340 g bulk pork breakfast sausage
	Vegetable oil or melted unsalted butter, as needed
2	tbsp unbleached all-purpose flour
2¼	cups/540 ml whole milk, plus more as needed
1	small bay leaf
	Pinch of ground nutmeg
	Fine sea salt and freshly ground black pepper
4	standard Classic Waffles (page 16), Buttermilk Waffles (page 18), or Golden Cornmeal Waffles (page 20), recrisped and warm (see Reviving Your Waffles, page 13)
1 or 2	green onions, green part only, thinly sliced on the diagonal
	Hot sauce, such as Tabasco, for serving

TO MAKE THE GRAVY: In a large frying pan over medium-high heat, cook the sausage, stirring occasionally and breaking it into rough ½-in/12-mm pieces with a wooden spoon, until the bits are well browned on the outside and no longer pink on the inside, 8 to 10 minutes. Adjust the heat as needed if the sausage is browning too quickly. Using a slotted spoon, transfer the sausage to a plate.

Pour off all but 2 tbsp fat from the frying pan, leaving any browned drippings in the pan; if you happen to have less than 2 tbsp fat, make up the difference with some oil. Set the frying pan over medium heat, whisk in the flour to make a roux, and cook for about 2 minutes. Whisking constantly, gradually pour in the milk. Once all the milk is in, add the bay leaf, increase the heat to medium-high, and bring the mixture to a boil. Reduce the heat to maintain a steady but not overly vigorous simmer and cook the gravy, whisking occasionally, until it is nicely thickened and the starchy taste of the flour has been cooked out, 5 to 6 minutes.

Return the sausage to the frying pan and add the nutmeg. Cook, stirring occasionally, until the sausage is heated through, about 3 minutes. Season the gravy with salt and pepper. (The gravy can be kept, covered, in the frying pan for 10 minutes or so; reheat it before serving and, if it has become too thick, thin it with additional milk.)

Divide the warm waffles among four individual plates. Discard the bay leaf from the gravy and spoon one-fourth of the gravy over each waffle. Garnish with the green onions and serve, passing hot sauce at the table.

CHAPTER 4
WAFFLE FINALES

Then there's dessert; my favorite part of any meal.

I have not figured out why waffles haven't gained acceptance as dessert. Perhaps it's because we think that indulgence or decadence should come at a higher cost than quick-to-make waffles embellished with a few simple toppings. Or maybe dessert's position in relation to breakfast is too close, and waffles' long-standing association with morning meals wins out.

I, for one, think waffles make exceptional desserts. Crisp-crusted and with an open crumb that soaks in whatever surrounds them, waffles have a true soul mate in ice cream—which is why you'll find several recipes in this chapter that put the two together. Fresh seasonal fruits, beautiful in color and scintillating in flavor, are also a natural pairing.

Some of the desserts in this chapter call for waffles from elsewhere in the book and offer tempting ways to use up leftovers; others include waffles tailor-made for the purpose. In many cases, one waffle can be swapped for another so long as the flavor profiles agree. So stop waffling—or maybe *start* waffling—and indulge in dessert.

WAFFLES BOSTOCK

MAKES **4** SERVINGS

The oddly named *bostock* is what many French *boulangères* make with day-old brioche—slices are slathered with frangipane (a butter-and-egg-laden almond cream), sprinkled with more almonds, and then baked until golden. True *bostock* is usually offered as breakfast or as a midday indulgence, but I think this waffle-based *bostock* is at its best topped with a scoop of ice cream and served as dessert. The contrast of crisp and creamy, and warm and cold, is nothing short of divine.

INGREDIENTS

FRANGIPANE

1	cup/100 g sliced skin-on almonds
½	cup/100 g sugar
⅛	tsp fine sea salt
1	large egg
½	tsp vanilla extract
¼	tsp almond extract
6	tbsp/85 g unsalted butter, at room temperature
4	standard Classic Waffles (page 16), Buttermilk Waffles (page 18), or Malted Waffles (page 19)
6	tbsp/115 g apricot or raspberry preserves
½	cup/50 g sliced skin-on almonds
	Confectioners' sugar, for serving
	Good-quality vanilla ice cream, for serving (optional)

Preheat the oven to 400°F/200°C/gas 6.

TO MAKE THE FRANGIPANE: In a food processor, pulse the almonds, sugar, and salt until the nuts are very finely chopped, then process continuously until the mixture is finely ground and meal-like, 15 to 20 seconds. Add the egg, vanilla, and almond extract and process until combined, about 10 seconds; the mixture may gather together into a ball. Using a rubber spatula, break up the ball and scrape the bottom and sides of the bowl. Add the butter and process until fully incorporated, about 10 seconds. Transfer the frangipane to a small bowl and stir to make sure it's well combined.

Line a baking sheet with parchment paper and lay the waffles on top. Spread 1½ tbsp of preserves evenly on each waffle, pushing it into the pockets. Spread one-quarter—about ⅓ cup/85 g—of the frangipane on each waffle, stopping just shy of the edge. Sprinkle each frangipane-topped waffle with 2 tbsp of the almonds.

Bake the waffles until the exposed edges are browned and crisped and the frangipane is golden and slightly puffed, 18 to 20 minutes. Sift confectioners' sugar over them and serve warm, topped with scoops of ice cream, if desired.

S'MORISH WAFFLES

MAKES **8** SERVINGS

This is a playful, open-faced spin on campfire s'mores that takes waffles as the graham cracker and billowy meringue as the marshmallow. Though they don't have the crunch or gooey factor of actual s'mores, I happen to think these little waffle confections taste even better because they're not so toothachingly sweet. Although milk chocolate is customary for s'mores, skip it here in favor of semisweet or bittersweet chocolate to really tone down the sugariness. For the sake of convenience, feel free to use semisweet or bittersweet chocolate chips instead of breaking up a chocolate bar.

INGREDIENTS

2	standard waffles, preferably Classic Waffles (page 16), Malted Waffles (page 19), or Peanut Butter Waffles (page 36), each one cut into quarters
4	oz/115 g bittersweet chocolate, preferably in candy-bar form, broken into chunks
1	egg white
	Pinch of cream of tartar
	Pinch of fine sea salt
½	cup/100 g sugar
1	tsp vanilla extract
	Cold milk, for serving (optional)

Preheat the oven to 425°F/220°C/gas 7. Line a rimmed baking sheet with parchment paper and lay the waffle pieces on top. Fill a medium saucepan with about 1 in/2.5 cm of water and bring the water to a bare simmer over medium heat.

Slide the baking sheet into the oven and warm the waffles for about 5 minutes, flipping each one about halfway through. Remove from the oven and top each waffle piece with about ½ oz/15 g chocolate, leaving a narrow border around the edge. Set them aside, but leave the oven on.

In the bowl of a stand mixer, combine the egg white, 2 tbsp water, cream of tartar, salt, and sugar and whisk well. Set the bowl on top of the saucepan (the bottom of the bowl should not touch the water), and whisk constantly until the sugar has dissolved and the mixture is frothy and feels very warm to the fingertip (if you have an instant-read thermometer, it should register about 125°F/52°C).

Remove the bowl from the pan and add the vanilla. Beat the mixture at medium-high speed, using a stand mixer fitted with the whisk attachment, until the mixture has cooled and a glossy, voluminous, soft-peak meringue forms, about 3 minutes.

Using two soupspoons, top each waffle piece with a cloud of meringue, covering the chocolate as best you can and anchoring the meringue to the waffle. (It's not necessary to achieve perfection.) Using the back of a spoon, create peaks and swirls in the meringue.

Bake the meringue-topped waffles until nicely browned, 2 to 4 minutes. Let cool for a few minutes. Serve with glasses of cold milk, if desired.

WAFFLES WITH SWEET GOAT CHEESE, CHERRIES IN PORT SYRUP, AND TOASTED ALMONDS

MAKES  4 SERVINGS

I'm drawn to goat cheese desserts like a moth to a flame—I love that blend of sweetness, saltiness, and funky tang. Succulent cherries are a splendid match for goat cheese because although they're sweet, they also have a certain savoriness about them that keeps them in line with the cheese. In fact, the quartet of headlining ingredients in this easy, elegant dessert—goat cheese, cherries, port, and almonds—have an affinity for one another, so even though each one is playing its own part, together they taste as if they were meant to be, well, together.

INGREDIENTS

CHERRIES IN PORT SYRUP

8	oz/225 g sweet red cherries, pitted and halved
1¼	cups/300 ml port
2	tbsp sugar
8 to 10	black peppercorns
1	strip orange zest, removed with a vegetable peeler
	Pinch of fine sea salt
One	1-in/2.5-cm piece vanilla bean, halved lengthwise, or ¼ tsp vanilla extract

SWEET GOAT CHEESE

4	oz/115 g fresh goat cheese (chèvre), crumbled
¼	cup/60 ml heavy cream
1	tbsp superfine sugar
2 or 3	standard Classic Waffles (page 16), Malted Waffles (page 19), or Belgian Waffles (page 22), recrisped and warm (see Reviving Your Waffles, page 13)
⅓	cup/30 g sliced almonds, toasted until *deeply* browned (see page 10)

TO MAKE THE CHERRIES IN PORT SYRUP: Place the cherries in a small bowl. In a small, heavy-bottomed saucepan, bring the port, sugar, peppercorns, orange zest, salt, and vanilla bean (if using) to a simmer over medium-high heat. Simmer, stirring occasionally, until lightly syrupy and reduced to a scant ½ cup/120 ml, about 10 minutes. Pour the mixture through a fine-mesh strainer over the cherries. (If using the vanilla extract, add it now.) Set the cherries aside for at least 1 hour to let the flavors meld. (Once cooled, the cherries can be covered and refrigerated for up to 6 hours; bring them to room temperature before serving.)

TO MAKE THE SWEET GOAT CHEESE: In the bowl of a stand mixer fitted with the whisk attachment or in a bowl with a handheld mixer, beat the goat cheese, cream, and sugar on medium-high speed, scraping down the bowl from time to time, until the sugar dissolves and the mixture is light and fluffy, about 2 minutes. (The goat cheese can be covered and refrigerated for up to 24 hours; bring it to room temperature and stir well before using.)

Cut the waffles into sections and set two or three pieces on each serving plate, overlapping them or arranging them in an attractive fashion. Spoon one-fourth of the goat cheese onto each serving. (If you like, make quenelles of goat cheese by using two spoons to form the cheese into an egg shape.) Top with a portion of cherries and drizzle with the port syrup. Sprinkle with one-fourth of the almonds and serve right away.

PECAN-BROWNED BUTTER WAFFLES WITH PEACHES AND BLACKBERRIES AND BOURBON CREAM

MAKES  4 SERVINGS

Pecans, peaches, and bourbon. All Southern, all delicious. Put them together in almost any configuration and there's really no way to go wrong. Here, with plump blackberries adding a punch of color to the peaches, and the bourbon making fiery a mixture of cream, crème fraîche, and brown sugar, things are very right. If you like, change things up a bit by substituting nectarines for the peaches and blueberries or raspberries for the blackberries.

INGREDIENTS

BOURBON CREAM

½	cup/120 ml heavy cream
½	cup/115 g crème fraîche
¼	cup/50 g packed dark brown sugar
1	tbsp bourbon

PEACHES AND BLACKBERRIES

1	lb/455 g firm, ripe yellow peaches, pitted and sliced ¼ in/6 mm thick
3	tbsp sugar
	Pinch of fine sea salt
1	cup/140 g blackberries
	Squeeze of fresh lemon juice
4	standard Pecan-Browned Butter Waffles (page 38), recrisped and warm (see Reviving Your Waffles, page 13)

TO MAKE THE BOURBON CREAM: Combine the heavy cream, crème fraîche, brown sugar, and bourbon in a medium bowl and whisk just until the sugar dissolves and the cream is thick and voluminous. Cover and refrigerate until needed.

TO MAKE THE PEACHES AND BLACKBERRIES: In a medium bowl, toss together the peaches, sugar, and salt until combined. Let stand, tossing gently once or twice, until the sugar dissolves and the peaches are glossy with the juice that they've released, 10 to 15 minutes. Add the blackberries and lemon juice and toss gently to combine.

Set a waffle on each plate. Top each with one-quarter of the fruit mixture and drizzle with any juices left over in the bowl. Spoon large dollops of the cream on top and serve right away.

BLACK SESAME WAFFLES WITH GREEN TEA ICE CREAM AND STRAWBERRY-SAKE COULIS

Senbei, Japanese rice crackers that are flavored with any number of sweet or savory seasonings, including sesame, were the inspiration for these waffles. Black sesame is a distinctly Asian flavor (to my palate, it's more robust tasting than white sesame), and its nutty notes play off the grassiness of the green tea and floral quality of the strawberries. This is a splashy, colorful dessert—mossy green ice cream, deep pink coulis, and black-flecked waffles make for a unique visual effect. I recommend baking the waffle batter at a medium or slightly higher setting for an extended time to get the waffles beautifully browned and crisped.

INGREDIENTS

COULIS

2	cups/340 g fresh ripe strawberries, hulled, or thawed frozen strawberries (not packed in syrup)
2	tbsp sugar, plus more as needed
2	tsp fresh lemon juice, plus more as needed
	Pinch of fine sea salt
1½	tbsp sake

WAFFLES

1	cup/140 g unbleached all-purpose flour
2½	tbsp sugar
1	tbsp black sesame seeds, toasted
1	tsp baking powder
¼	tsp fine sea salt
1	large egg
1	cup/240 ml whole milk, at room temperature
2	tbsp/30 g unsalted butter, melted and cooled slightly
1	tbsp toasted sesame oil
2	pt/960 ml green tea ice cream
	Black sesame seeds, toasted, for garnish

TO MAKE THE COULIS: Cut the berries in half so that they'll purée more easily, and drop them into a blender. Add the sugar, lemon juice, and salt and purée until smooth. Strain into a bowl to remove the seeds. Taste the coulis and add more sugar and/or lemon juice, if needed. Stir in the sake, cover, and refrigerate until you're ready to serve.

TO MAKE THE WAFFLES: Set a large wire rack on a large, rimmed baking sheet. Preheat a standard (not Belgian) waffle iron; a medium to medium-high setting along with a longer baking time will work best for getting the waffles nicely browned and extra-crisp.

In a medium bowl, whisk together the flour, sugar, sesame seeds, baking powder, and salt and until well combined.

In a small bowl, whisk the egg until combined, and then whisk in the milk. Gradually whisk in the butter, followed by the sesame oil.

Pour the liquid ingredients into the dry ingredients and whisk gently just until the batter is evenly moistened.

Pour ½ cup/120 ml of the batter (or the waffler manufacturer's recommended amount) into the center of the waffle iron. Use a rubber spatula to spread the batter to about ½ in/12 mm from the waffler's edge. Close the lid and bake the waffle until the waffler indicates that it's done (it's probably neither browned nor crisp enough). Open the lid to check on the browning, and then continue to bake until the waffle is deep golden brown and very crisp; this will likely take several extra minutes.

Remove the waffle and set it on the wire rack. Bake the remaining batter in the same fashion, transferring each waffle to the rack. Cut the waffles into smaller wedges or triangles for serving like cookies.

Scoop the ice cream into six to eight individual bowls. Spoon chilled coulis over each serving and garnish with a sprinkling of sesame seeds. Tuck two or three waffle pieces (depending on their size) into each bowl and serve right away.

VARIATION

BLACK SESAME MINI WAFFLES

If you're so inclined, instead of full-size waffles, you can make mini waffles to serve alongside the ice cream. The batter will yield 40 to 45 mini waffles—more than you'll need, but the leftovers freeze well and can be crisped in the oven or in a toaster.

Using a 1-tbsp measuring spoon and working quickly, pour about 2 tsp batter into the center of each quadrant, rectangle, or square that makes up the larger grid of the waffle iron—the amount of batter will seem extremely scant. Close the lid and bake the waffles until well browned and crisp. It may take a couple of rounds to get the size of the mini waffles just right. Transfer the waffles to the wire rack and repeat with the remaining batter.

SUMMER BERRY AND WAFFLE PUDDINGS

This is a dessert for the height of summer, when berries are abundant and in their prime. The fruit is really the star here, and the waffles, which replace the bread that's used in traditional summer pudding, literally play a supporting role—they're staled and layered into ramekins with the macerated berries. Unmolded, the puddings are absolutely stunning, and served with voluptuous sweet-tangy cream, they sing deliciously of the season. This is a fine way to put leftover waffles to use, or to use the ones in the freezer that have lost their good looks.

INGREDIENTS

PUDDINGS

1	lb/455 g strawberries, hulled and sliced thin
1	cup/140 g raspberries
1	cup/140 g blueberries
1	cup/140 g blackberries
½	cup/100 g sugar
	Pinch of fine sea salt
2	tbsp fresh lemon juice
4 to 6	standard Classic Waffles (page 16), Buttermilk Waffles (page 18), Belgian Waffles (page 22), or Malted Waffles (page 19)

SOUR CREAM WHIPPED CREAM

⅔	cup/165 ml heavy cream
⅓	cup/75 ml sour cream
2	tbsp sugar

TO MAKE THE PUDDINGS: In a large saucepan, combine all the berries, sugar, and salt. Set the pan over medium-high heat and warm the berries, stirring occasionally and very gently, just until they release some of their juices and the sugar dissolves, about 4 minutes. The mixture should not reach a simmer or be hot throughout. Add the lemon juice, then transfer to a large bowl and let cool to room temperature.

Meanwhile, rinse the insides of six 5-oz/150-ml ramekins with water to moisten them, then line each one with plastic wrap, letting the excess overhang the rim. (Moistening the insides of the ramekins will allow the plastic wrap to slide against the surface rather than stick relentlessly, so that lining them will be easier.) Set the ramekins on a rimmed baking sheet or in a baking dish large enough to hold them in a single layer.

Using a round cookie cutter just a bit smaller than the insides of the ramekins, stamp out 12 rounds from the waffles. If needed, trim the uneven edges and push the scraps together to create a piecemeal waffle from which more rounds can be cut.

Pour a generous 1 cup/240 ml of the berry juices that have collected in the bowl into a small, shallow bowl. Spoon about ⅓ cup/60 g berries into each ramekin; the berries should completely cover the bottom. Working one at a time, quickly dip both sides of six waffle rounds in the berry juices and set one round in each ramekin. Spoon the remaining berries into the ramekins, dividing them evenly and mounding them up. Dip the remaining six waffle rounds in the berry juices and set one on top of each pile of berries, pressing down firmly to compress; the ramekins' contents will stand quite high over the rims of the ramekins. Drizzle any remaining berry juices over the waffle rounds.

Fold the overhanging plastic wrap to enclose the puddings. Set a second baking sheet or baking dish on top of the puddings, and then place weights on top—a few heavy cans or bottles work well. Refrigerate the puddings for at least 12 hours or up to 24 hours.

TO MAKE THE WHIPPED CREAM: When you're ready to serve, in a bowl of a stand mixer fitted with the whisk attachment or in a bowl using a handheld mixer, beat together the cream, sour cream, and sugar on medium-high speed until thick and voluminous.

Open the plastic wrap covering each pudding. Invert the puddings onto serving plates and peel off the plastic wrap. Tidy up the plates by wiping any messy juices with paper towels. Spoon a generous dollop of whipped cream on each pudding and serve right away.

PARFAITS OF WAFFLE CROUTONS, VANILLA GELATO, AND PEPPERED STRAWBERRIES WITH BALSAMIC REDUCTION

MAKES  4 SERVINGS

In the summer, fresh strawberries macerated with sugar and black pepper spooned over vanilla gelato and drizzled with balsamic syrup becomes my house dessert. This version includes toasted waffle cubes that add a welcome element of crunch—much like a waffle cone, deconstructed. You can use vanilla ice cream in place of gelato, but I think the lighter flavor and softer, stickier texture of gelato is a better match for the berries and balsamic. Vanilla frozen yogurt is a superb option, too.

INGREDIENTS

3	cups/115 g diced (½-in/12-mm) waffles, preferably Classic Waffles (page 16), Buttermilk Waffles (page 18), or Malted Waffles (page 19)
½	cup/120 ml balsamic vinegar
2	cups/340 g strawberries, hulled and thinly sliced
2 to 3	tbsp sugar
½	tsp freshly ground black pepper
1½	pt/720 ml good-quality vanilla gelato

Preheat the oven to 375°F/190°C/gas 5.

Distribute the waffle cubes in an even layer on a rimmed baking sheet. Bake, stirring a couple of times, until the cubes are deeply golden and crisp, about 12 minutes. Set aside to cool.

In a small, nonreactive saucepan over medium heat, simmer the vinegar until glossy, thickened, and reduced to a generous 3 tbsp, about 10 minutes. Pour the reduced vinegar into a small, nonreactive bowl and let it cool to room temperature; it should be thick and syrupy when cooled.

While the vinegar cools, in a medium bowl, gently toss the strawberries with the sugar (use 2 tbsp if the berries are sweet, or up to 3 tbsp if they're on the tart side) and pepper until combined. Let stand until the sugar dissolves and the berries soften a bit and release some juice, 5 to 10 minutes; stir once or twice to ensure that the sugar dissolves.

Place about a scant ¼ cup/7 g toasted waffle cubes in the bottom of each of four serving glasses or compotes. Top the cubes with a scoop of gelato. Add a few generous spoonfuls of berries and juice over the gelato and drizzle with about 2 tsp balsamic syrup. Repeat the layering, using up the remaining ingredients and finishing with balsamic syrup. Serve the parfaits right away.

CHOCOLATE STOUT WAFFLE SUNDAES

MAKES 4 TO 6 SERVINGS

Bitten by the beer waffle bug (see Amber Ale Waffles, page 46), my husband requested a chocolate stout waffle dessert, so consider this devilish concoction his brainchild. With so many ingredients from the deep, dark, roasty-toasty end of the flavor spectrum working in unison, these sundaes are things of serious deliciousness. Chocolate stout is made with darkly roasted "chocolate" malt; some versions actually list cocoa as a flavoring. If you can't find chocolate stout, regular stout (also called Irish stout), oatmeal stout, or cream stout are all reasonable substitutes.

INGREDIENTS

WAFFLES

1	cup/140 g unbleached all-purpose flour
1½	tsp baking powder
¼	tsp fine sea salt
1	large egg
½	tsp vanilla extract
¾	cup/180 ml chocolate stout
4	tbsp/55 g unsalted butter, melted and cooled slightly
2	tbsp packed light or dark brown sugar
1 to 1½	pt/480 to 720 ml good-quality vanilla or coffee ice cream
	Bittersweet Chocolate Sauce (page 101), Burnt Caramel Sauce (page 100), or both, warmed
	Whipped Cream (page 90)
	Chopped smoked almonds

Preheat the oven to 225°F/110°C/gas ¼ and set a large wire rack on a large, rimmed baking sheet.

TO MAKE THE WAFFLES: Preheat your waffle iron.

In a medium bowl, whisk together the flour, baking powder, and salt until well combined.

In a small bowl, whisk the egg and vanilla until combined, and then whisk in the stout. Pour in the butter, add the brown sugar, and whisk until dissolved.

Pour the liquid ingredients into the dry ingredients and whisk gently just until the batter is evenly moistened. It's fine if some small lumps remain.

Pour ½ cup/120 ml of the batter (or the waffler manufacturer's recommended amount) into the center of the waffle iron. Use a rubber spatula to spread the batter to about ½ in/12 mm from the waffler's edge. Close the lid and bake the waffle until dark golden brown.

Remove the waffle and set it on the wire rack. Slide the baking sheet into the oven to keep the waffle warm. Bake the remaining batter, transferring each waffle to the rack in the oven.

Cut the waffles into sections and arrange as many as you'd like on individual serving plates or in bowls. Top the waffles with scoops of ice cream and drizzle with chocolate or caramel sauce (or both). Dollop whipped cream on top and sprinkle with chopped smoked almonds. Serve right away.

CHAPTER 5

TO TOP IT OFF

I was eight or nine years old and on a family vacation in New England the first time I tasted pure maple syrup (in our house, we only ever used "syrup" of the unspecified type on pancakes and waffles). Since then, I've never wanted anything *but* maple syrup on my waffles and pancakes. Not even pats of butter. That's how much and for how long I've been smitten with maple syrup. I don't make maple syrup infusions with fruits or nuts or spices because I'm not one to fool with perfection, especially when perfection costs as much as it does.

Maple syrup may be my favorite way to dress a breakfast waffle, but of course it isn't the only way. The trick is that whatever you put on a waffle shouldn't turn it soggy on contact—rather, a topping should soften and enrich the waffle just enough to give it an irresistible succulence. In this chapter, you'll find a selection of recipes for topping options, from breakfast-appropriate flavored butters and berry compote to spirited fruits and sumptuous sauces that turn humble waffles into distinctive desserts.

HONEY BUTTER WITH ORANGE ESSENCE

MAKES ABOUT ¹/₂ CUP / 225 G

For those times when all you want is a simple finishing touch on your waffles, not a sugary syrup or scene-stealing fruit, there's this lightly sweetened butter. It doesn't require much effort to make but will elevate a plain waffle to special-breakfast status. The butter, with its orange essence, is an excellent partner to most types of waffles, even ones with big personalities like Golden Cornmeal Waffles (page 20) and Buckwheat-Sour Cream Waffles (page 43).

INGREDIENTS

6	tbsp/85 g unsalted butter, at room temperature
2	tbsp honey
1	tbsp fresh orange juice
¼	tsp grated orange zest, minced
	Pinch of fine sea salt

In a small bowl, whisk together all ingredients until well combined. (The butter will keep, covered, in the refrigerator for up to 1 week. Bring to room temperature before serving.)

VARIATION

MOLASSES-ORANGE BUTTER

The molasses in this butter imparts a deep, slightly smoky, bittersweet flavor that works especially well with Golden Cornmeal Waffles (page 20), Spicy Pumpkin Waffles (page 34), Toasted Oatmeal Waffles with a Hint of Cinnamon (page 40), and Anadama Waffles with Currants (page 44).

Follow the master recipe, substituting 2 tbsp mild molasses for the honey and omitting the orange juice.

MAPLE CREAM CHEESE

MAKES ABOUT **1¹/₂ CUPS** / **340** G

This waffle topping has luscious texture and a sweet, savory, and tangy flavor that makes me want to eat if off a spoon. Grade B maple syrup yields the best results here because it's thick, dark, and intensely flavored. Grade A dark amber is the second choice; I don't recommend using a lighter maple syrup than those. Maple Cream Cheese alone on top of a waffle is delicious, or it can be paired with Gingery Cranberry-Pineapple Syrup (page 95) or used instead of whipped cream to accompany fresh fruit.

In a stand mixer with the whisk attachment or in a medium bowl with a handheld mixer, beat the cream cheese and butter until fluffy and smooth, scraping down the sides of the bowl as needed. Add the confectioners' sugar and beat until well combined. Scrape down the bowl and add the maple syrup and vanilla and beat until incorporated. The mixture will be quite soft, like thick sour cream. Cover and refrigerate until needed. (The cream cheese will keep, refrigerated, for up to 2 weeks; stir to recombine if the maple separates out to the bottom.)

INGREDIENTS

8	oz/225 g cream cheese, at room temperature
2	tbsp/30 g unsalted butter, at room temperature
2	tbsp confectioners' sugar
¹/₃	cup/75 ml pure maple syrup, preferably grade B (see recipe introduction)
¼	tsp vanilla extract

VARIATION

MAPLE CREAM CHEESE WITH SMOKED PAPRIKA

Here smoked paprika infuses the cream cheese with an intriguing savoriness and lovely flecks of brick-red color. It's especially good on Peanut Butter Waffles (page 36), Spicy Pumpkin Waffles (page 34), and Pecan-Browned Butter Waffles (page 38).

Follow the master recipe , adding ½ tsp sweet smoked paprika along with the confectioners' sugar.

WHIPPED CREAM

MAKES ABOUT 2 CUPS / 480 G

If you can find some, use heavy cream that is labeled "pasteurized" rather than "ultrapasteurized." The difference in flavor is noticeable, with the former having a sweeter, fresher, more buttery taste because it's processed more gently than the latter (which is why it also has a shorter shelf life). If you're using the whipped cream on a dessert, you can spike it with a tablespoon of spirit—bourbon, dark rum, or brandy are top choices—but use one that complements the flavors in the dish.

In the bowl of a stand mixer fitted with the whisk attachment or in a bowl with a handheld mixer, beat all the ingredients on medium speed until the cream is lightly thickened. Increase the speed to high and beat until the cream holds soft peaks when the mixer is lifted. Use right away or cover and refrigerate for up to 12 hours; rewhisk gently before serving.

INGREDIENTS

1	cup/240 ml cold heavy cream
1	tbsp sugar
½	tsp vanilla extract (optional)

LEMON CURD

MAKES ABOUT 1²/₃ CUPS / 470 G

Thick, silky, egg-rich lemon curd is sublime on freshly baked scones, so why not on waffles? I'm not one for lemony concoctions that are so sour they make the taste buds bristle, nor ones that are cloyingly sweet. For me, this formula yields a curd that strikes a perfectly pleasing sweet-tart balance. Use only lemon juice that you've squeezed yourself; the bottled variety lacks the crisp, vibrant flavor of fresh. It may seem daft to add grated lemon zest to the hot curd only to strain it out a minute later, but the warmth releases the zest's essential oils, not its bitterness, and straining leaves the curd lusciously smooth.

INGREDIENTS	
3	egg yolks
1	large egg
¾	cup plus 2 tbsp/175 g sugar
	Pinch of fine sea salt
½	cup/120 ml fresh lemon juice
1	tbsp finely grated lemon zest
6	tbsp/85 g unsalted butter, cut into 6 pieces

In a small, nonreactive saucepan, whisk the egg yolks and whole egg until combined. Add the sugar and salt and whisk until the mixture is homogeneous. Whisk in the lemon juice and set the pan over medium heat. Cook, stirring constantly with a heatproof rubber spatula and scraping along the bottom and sides, until the mixture takes on a translucent quality, has thickened enough to lightly coat a metal spoon, and registers 170°F/77°C on an instant-read thermometer; it will be quite saucy at this point. Don't let the mixture reach a simmer; if it does, the curd will, well, curdle.

Remove the pan from the heat and immediately stir in the zest. Whisk in the butter, one piece at a time, and when all the butter has been incorporated, pour the curd through a fine-mesh strainer set over a bowl. Press on the zest in the strainer to extract as much curd from it as possible.

Lay plastic wrap directly against the surface of the curd to prevent a skin from forming and refrigerate until the curd is chilled and set, at least 2 hours. (The curd will keep, refrigerated, for up to 2 weeks.)

CONTINUED >

VARIATION

LIME CURD

Each time I make lime curd, I hope that it'll magically turn out to be pale green in color, and then am a wee bit disappointed when it finishes almost as sunny yellow as lemon curd. Its flavor, however—more bracing and exotic than lemon—makes up for its copycat looks.

Follow the master recipe, substituting freshly squeezed lime juice and grated lime zest for the lemon juice and zest.

LEMON CURD OR LIME CURD MOUSSELINE

Folding whipped cream into citrus curd lightens its texture and tames its intensity. Lemon Curd Mousseline is especially good dolloped onto Wild Blueberry-Buttermilk Waffles (page 30); Lime Curd Mousseline is a natural with Coconut[2] Waffles (page 32).

Measure ½ cup/140 g chilled curd into a medium, nonreactive bowl. In another bowl, with a whisk, rotary beater, or handheld mixer, beat ½ cup/120 ml heavy cream, 2 tsp sugar, and ⅛ tsp vanilla extract until the cream holds soft peaks when the whisk or mixer is lifted. Using a rubber spatula, fold the whipped cream into the curd. Cover and refrigerate until well chilled, about 1 hour. The mousseline will keep in the refrigerator for up to 5 days. Makes about 1⅔ cups/405 ml.

BLUEBERRY COMPOTE

MAKES ABOUT 2¼ CUPS / 540 G

Warm blueberry compote spooned over Buttermilk Waffles (page 18), Classic Waffles (page 16), Belgian Waffles (page 22), or Golden Cornmeal Waffles (page 20) will satisfy any blueberry waffle devotee. (I know because I'm married to one.) As a final flourish to compote-topped waffles, I like a big spoonful of sour cream sweetened with a little sugar—the rich tanginess of the sour cream is a perfect complement to the berries.

INGREDIENTS

6	tbsp/70 g sugar, plus more as needed
1	tsp cornstarch
	Pinch of fine sea salt
3	cups/455 g fresh or frozen blueberries
2	tbsp water
1	tbsp fresh lemon juice

In a medium, nonreactive saucepan, whisk together the sugar, cornstarch, and salt until well combined. Add the blueberries and water and bring to a simmer over medium-high heat, stirring occasionally. Cook until the berries release their juice and the juice is glossy, translucent, and lightly thickened, about 5 minutes. Remove from the heat and stir in the lemon juice. Taste the compote and add sugar, ½ tsp at a time, as needed to heighten the sweetness.

Transfer the compote to a bowl and let cool. Serve warm or at room temperature. (The compote will keep in an airtight container in the refrigerator for up to 3 days. Rewarm gently before serving.)

GINGERY CRANBERRY-PINEAPPLE SYRUP

MAKES ABOUT 2 CUPS / 480 ML

Cranberries contain a lot of pectin, and pectin gives this crimson-colored syrup its body and viscosity. The flavors here are quite assertive, so this syrup is particularly well suited to waffles with nutty or spicy profiles, ones such as Honeyed Whole-Wheat Waffles (page 25), Pecan-Browned Butter Waffles (page 38), Peanut Butter Waffles (page 36), and Spicy Pumpkin Waffles (page 34). Maple Cream Cheese (page 89) pairs perfectly with this syrup on top of waffles, and together they're a stunning color contrast.

INGREDIENTS

1½	cups/300g sugar
¼	cup/60 ml water
12	oz/340 g fresh or frozen cranberries
1½	cups/360 ml pineapple juice, preferably not from concentrate
	Pinch of fine sea salt
1½	tbsp grated fresh ginger

Pour the sugar into a large, heavy-bottomed, non-reactive saucepan, shake the pan to distribute the sugar into an even layer, and add the water. Set the pan over medium-high heat and bring the mixture to a vigorous simmer, stirring only once or twice with a clean wooden spoon or heatproof rubber spatula to help the sugar dissolve. Once the sugar dissolves, continue simmering; the sugar will begin to take on a golden hue—once it does, swirl the pan occasionally to encourage even browning. Cook the sugar until golden amber in color, about 8 minutes from the point at which the mixture reached a vigorous simmer.

Remove the pan from the heat and carefully add the cranberries, pineapple juice, and salt; the mixture will bubble and hiss energetically, so use caution. Return the pan to medium-high heat and bring to a simmer, stirring occasionally and getting into the pan corners to help the hardened caramel dissolve. Cook until there are no longer any lumps of caramel and the cranberries are fully softened and many have popped open, about 6 minutes.

Working in batches if needed, pour the mixture into a fine-mesh strainer set over a bowl. With a rubber spatula, push down on the solids in the strainer to extract as much liquid and pulp as possible; from time to time, scrape the bottom of the strainer, letting the purée fall into the bowl. Discard the solids in the strainer. Add the ginger to the strainer and push down on the solids with the spatula, letting the juice fall into the bowl. Whisk the syrup until smooth. The syrup will keep in an airtight container in the refrigerator for up to 2 weeks. It will gel with chilling; reheat, whisking, to liquefy the syrup, adding a bit more pineapple juice as needed if it's too thick.

MULTI-BERRY COULIS

MAKES ABOUT 2 CUPS / 480 ML

A coulis is simply a smooth purée, usually of uncooked fruit, that's served as a sauce. In the summer months, fresh berries are the obvious choice to use, but when berries aren't in season—and even if they are—frozen mixed berries are a great option. Depending on how you're serving the coulis, you can stir in flavorings for added interest. For example, if the coulis is accompanying waffles at breakfast or brunch, you might stir in a tablespoon or two of fresh orange juice to add a citrusy twist or a squeeze of fresh ginger juice for piquancy; if it's topping a dessert waffle, you might spike it with orange liqueur, framboise, kirsch, or—my favorite—good-quality cachaça.

In a blender, purée the berries, sugar, and salt until smooth. Work the purée through a fine-mesh strainer into a bowl. Discard the seeds and skins in the strainer.

Stir in the lemon juice. Taste the coulis and add more sugar as desired to heighten the sweetness. Cover and refrigerate until needed. (Coulis will keep in an airtight container in the refrigerator for up to 3 days.)

INGREDIENTS

4	cups/455 g mixed fresh or thawed frozen hulled strawberries, raspberries, blueberries, and blackberries
¼	cup/50 g sugar, plus more as needed
	Pinch of fine sea salt
1	tbsp fresh lemon juice

SAUTÉED APPLES IN HARD CIDER

MAKES ABOUT 3 CUPS / 570 G, ENOUGH FOR 4 OR 5 SERVINGS

Buttery sautéed apples with a soupçon of spice are an easy waffle accoutrement that's especially good in the autumn and winter months. The hard cider, reduced down and barely thickened with cornstarch, yields a syrup that keeps the apples lush and soaks ever so slightly into the waffle. If the apples are completing a breakfast waffle, garnish each serving with a generous dollop of crème fraîche—its richness and tanginess are the perfect complement to the fruit. On a dessert waffle, vanilla ice cream melting onto the warm apples would be hard to beat.

INGREDIENTS

3	tbsp unsalted butter
4	Golden Delicious apples (about 1½ lb/ 680 g), peeled, cored, and sliced ¼ in/ 6 mm thick
⅛	tsp ground cinnamon
	Pinch of ground nutmeg
	Fine sea salt
1½	cups/360 ml hard apple or pear cider
⅓	cup/65 g packed light brown sugar
½	tsp cornstarch
1	tsp water
1	tbsp fresh lemon juice

In a large frying pan over high heat, heat the butter until foamy. Add the apples, cinnamon, nutmeg, and a pinch of salt. Cook, tossing occasionally, until the apples are softened and golden, about 7 minutes. Transfer the apples to a bowl.

Return the frying pan to high heat and add the hard cider, brown sugar, and another pinch of salt. Simmer vigorously, scraping up any browned bits with a wooden spoon, until the cider is reduced to ¾ cup/180 ml, 4 to 5 minutes. Meanwhile, in a small bowl, combine the cornstarch and water.

When the cider is reduced, stir the cornstarch slurry to recombine, and then stir it into the cider. Bring the mixture to a simmer, stirring, and cook until lightly thickened and glossy; this will probably take only 30 seconds or so. Stir in the lemon juice.

Return the apples, along with any accumulated juice, to the frying pan and turn down the heat to medium. Cook, stirring gently, just until the apples are moistened and heated through, 1 to 2 minutes. Serve warm.

BUTTER-RUM BANANAS

MAKES ABOUT **4** SERVINGS

This ultra-rich, downright decadent topping could not be any easier to make. Pair it with Coconut[2] Waffles (page 32) and you'll have a dessert with perfectly harmonious tropical flavors. But Pecan-Browned Butter Waffles (page 38), Peanut Butter Waffles (page 36), or even Classic Waffles (page 16) or Malted Waffles (page 19) are delicious matches, too. Whichever waffles you choose, first top them with good-quality vanilla ice cream, then spoon the warm bananas and sauce over the top. Yum.

In a large frying pan over medium heat, melt the butter. Add the brown sugar and salt and stir until evenly moistened. Pour in the rum, turn up the heat to medium-high, and whisk to combine. Simmer, whisking frequently, until the mixture is slightly thickened and syrupy and no longer smells fiery with alcohol, 2 to 3 minutes. Stir in the vanilla, and then add the bananas. Cook, gently turning the banana slices with a heatproof rubber spatula, just until the bananas are heated through, about 2 minutes. Serve warm.

INGREDIENTS

4	tbsp/55 g unsalted butter
½	cup/100 g packed light brown sugar
	Big pinch of fine sea salt
⅓	cup/75 ml dark rum
½	tsp vanilla extract
3	medium-large firm bananas, peeled and sliced ½ in/12 mm thick on the diagonal

BURNT CARAMEL SAUCE

MAKES ABOUT **1½ CUPS** / **360** ML

The transformation of one-dimensionally sweet granulated sugar into thick, smoky, bittersweet caramel is truly a marvel of science. That caramel is made so easily with so few ingredients and tastes so wondrously good does not go unappreciated in my kitchen, even after hundreds of batches. Salted caramel is au courant these days—feel free to add as much salt as you like to this sauce and call it "salty caramel" or "sea salt caramel" if you're looking for a name with a bit more cachet.

INGREDIENTS

1	cup/200 g sugar
¼	cup/60 ml water
1	cup/240 ml heavy cream
3	tbsp unsalted butter
¼	tsp vanilla extract
	Big pinch of fine sea salt, or more to taste

Pour the sugar into a medium, heavy-bottomed saucepan, shake the pan to distribute the sugar into an even layer, and add the water. Set the pan over medium-high heat and bring the mixture to a vigorous simmer, stirring only once or twice with a clean wooden spoon or heatproof rubber spatula to help the sugar dissolve. Once the sugar dissolves, continue simmering; the sugar will begin to take on a golden hue—once it does, swirl the pan occasionally to encourage even browning. Cook the sugar until deep reddish brown in color and smoking lightly, about 10 minutes from the point at which the mixture reached a vigorous simmer.

Remove the pan from the heat and carefully pour in the cream; the mixture will steam and bubble energetically, so use caution. Set the pan over medium-low heat and stir well, getting into the pan's corners, until the hardened caramelized sugar fully dissolves; this may take some time and quite a lot of stirring.

Remove the pan from the heat and stir in the butter, vanilla, and salt until the butter is incorporated. Using a spoon, taste the caramel—it may still be hot, so be careful!—and add more salt if desired.

Transfer the sauce to a bowl and let cool. Serve warm. (The sauce will keep in an airtight container in the refrigerator for up to 3 weeks. Rewarm gently before serving.)

BITTERSWEET CHOCOLATE SAUCE

MAKES ABOUT 2 CUPS / 480 ML

Homemade chocolate sauce is dead easy to make and can instantly turn ice cream—on a waffle or not—into a full-fledged dessert. This explains why there's always a container in my refrigerator. (But it doesn't explain why there always appear to be small spoonfuls missing from the chilled mass.) To state the obvious, use the best-quality bittersweet chocolate that you can bear to purchase—the difference can be tasted in the finished sauce.

INGREDIENTS
1 cup/240 ml heavy cream
¼ cup/60 ml light corn syrup
Big pinch of fine sea salt
6 oz/170 g bittersweet chocolate (preferably with 70 percent cocoa solids), chopped
2 tbsp unsalted butter

In a small saucepan over medium-high heat, bring the cream, corn syrup, and salt to a boil, stirring once or twice to ensure that the corn syrup is incorporated into the cream. When the mixture reaches a boil, turn off the heat and add the chocolate and butter. Let stand for a minute or two, then gently whisk until the mixture is smooth and homogeneous.

Transfer the sauce to a bowl and let cool. Serve warm. (The sauce will keep in an airtight container in the refrigerator for up to 2 weeks. Rewarm gently before serving.)

INDEX

W

ACKNOWLEDGMENTS

Many thanks to my mother, Barbara, who has supported me in all my endeavors, and whose Mickey Mouse pancakes were terrific, but whose perfectly crisp, browned waffles I always loved more.

Adam Ried, former *Cook's Illustrated* officemate and fellow air conditioning enthusiast, how can I repay you for testing waffle recipes in New England summer heat and humidity while your kitchen was under construction?

Friend and former *Cook's*-er Sandra Wu hosted a Weekend Waffle Fest to test a handful of recipes and feed friends and family. Thank you for being so thorough and quick.

Shaul Teplinsky and Joe Hao, friends and neighbors, were always game for tasting waffles, even the experimental ones, and even at midnight. Thank you for lending your taste buds, and for giving a home to waffles in need.

My dear friend Kay Rentschler creates food and prose that I aspire to. *Danke sehr* for always keeping me on my toes. Glenn Roberts of Anson Mills, I'm so glad Kay found you and that you're a part of our lives. Your grains kick all other grains' butt.

To Christyan, my husband and co-owner of two of the cutest French bulldogs ever: Thank you for putting up with me. And you're right, we do have it good.

And last but not least, I'd like to thank Lorena Jones and Amy Treadwell at Chronicle Books for giving me the opportunity to do this little book. It's been great fun, and I'm looking forward to the next one.